Expertise versus Respons
Children's Worlds

Education Policy Perspectives

General Editor: Professor Ivor Goodson, Warner Graduate School, University of Rochester, USA and Centre for Applied Research in Education, University of East Anglia, Norwich, UK

Education policy analysis has long been a neglected area in the UK and, to an extent, in the USA and Australia. The result has been a profound gap between the study of education and the formulation of education policy. For practitioners, such a lack of analysis of new policy initiatives has worrying implications, particularly at a time of such policy flux and change. Education policy has, in recent years, been a matter for intense political debate – the political and public interest in the working of the system has come at the same time as the breaking of the consensus on education policy by the New Right. As never before, political parties and pressure groups differ in their articulated policies and prescriptions for the education sector. Critical thinking about these developments is clearly imperative.

All those working within the system also need information on policy-making, policy implementation and effective day-to-day operation. Pressure on schools from government, education authorities and parents has generated an enormous need for knowledge among those on the receiving end of educational policies.

This Falmer Press series aims to fill the academic gap, to reflect the politicalization of education, and to provide the practitioners with the analysis for informed implementation of policies that they will need. It offers studies in broad areas of policy studies, with a particular focus on the following areas: school organization and improvement; critical social analysis; policy studies and evaluation; and education training.

Expertise versus Responsiveness in Children's Worlds: Politics in School, Home and Community Relationships

The 1996 Yearbook of the Politics of Education Association

Edited by

Maureen McClure

University of Pittsburgh

and

Jane Clark Lindle

University of Kentucky

 The Falmer Press

(A member of the Taylor & Francis Group)
Washington, DC • London

UK   Falmer Press, 1 Gunpowder Square, London, EC4A 3DE
USA   Falmer Press, Taylor & Francis Inc., 1900 Frost Road, Suite 101,
Bristol, PA 19007

First published in 1997

A catalogue record for this book is available from the British Library

Library of Congress Cataloguing-in-Publication Data are available on request

ISBN 0 7507 06678 cased
ISBN 0 7507 06686 paper

Jacket design by Caroline Archer

Typeset by Keyword Typesetting Services Ltd, Wallington, Surrey, printed in Great Britain by Henry Ling Limited on paper which has a specified pH value on final paper manufacture of not less than 7.5 and is therefore 'acid free'.

Every effort has been made to contact copyright holders for their permission to reprint material in this book. The publishers would be grateful to hear from any copyright holder who is not here acknowledged and will undertake to rectify any errors or omissions in future editions of this book.

Contents

Politics of Education Association

Yearbook Sponsor

The **Politics of Education Association (PEA)** promotes the development and dissemination of research and debate on educational policy and politics. PEA brings together scholars, practitioners and policy makers interested in educational governance and politics. It is affiliated as a Special Interest Group with the American Educational Research Association (AERA), and meets each spring in conjunction with AERA's annual meeting. PEA also sponsors its own biennial conferences on current policy issues in education in the fall. The annual membership dues for PEA are $US25.00 (subject to change). Members receive a copy of the annual *Yearbook* and the *Politics of Education Bulletin*, which includes news on member activities and occasional short scholarly pieces. Membership dues should be sent to **Louise Adler, PEA Treasurer, EC 552, Educational Administration, California State University, Fullerton, CA 92634–8000, USA**.

Previous PEA *Yearbooks* and their editors are:

The Politics of Excellence and Choice in Education
William Boyd and Charles Kerchner (1987)

The Politics of Reforming School Administration
Jane Hannaway and Robert Crowson (1988)

Education Politics for the New Century
Douglas Mitchell and Margaret Goertz (1989)

Politics of Curriculum and Testing
Susan Fuhrman and Betty Malen (1990)

The Politics of Urban Education in the United States
James G. Cibulka, Rodney J. Reed, and Kenneth K. Wong (1991)

The New Politics of Race and Gender
Catherine Marshall (1992)

The Politics of Linking Schools and Social Services
Louise Adler and Sid Gardner (1993)

The Study of Educational Politics
Jay D. Scribner and Donald H. Layton (1994)

**The Politics of Education and the New Institutionalism:
Reinventing the American School**
Robert L. Crowson, William Lowe Boyd and Hanne B. Mawhinney (1995)

About the Editors and Contributors

Duane Covrig is an Assistant Professor of Ethical Studies at Loma Linda University and a doctoral student in education at University of California, Riverside. His recent publications are on moral leadership and educational ethics, while his doctoral research is on organizational development and institutional theory. His research interests are in applied ethics, specifically organizational ethics.

Alan DeYoung is Professor of Education Policy Studies and Evaluation at the University of Kentucky, where his speciality is in Rural Education Politics and Policy and Appalachian studies. His most recent book *The Life and Death of a Rural American High School* (Garland, 1995). He was named 'Researcher of the Year' by the national Rural Education Association for this work and several journal articles based on the same fieldwork. Most recently, he completed a Fulbright Teaching and Lecturing Grant in the former Soviet republic of Kazakstan. He has several works in composition or in press from his studies there.

Benjamin Levin is Dean of Continuing Education and Professor of Educational Administration at the University of Manitoba. He has also worked as a senior government official and as a school district research director. His most recent book, also with J. A. Riffel, is *Schools and the Changing World* (Falmer, 1997).

Jane Clark Lindle is an Associate Professor in Educational Administration at the University of Kentucky. She recently served as the Interim Director of the University of Kentucky Institute on Education Reform and is currently co-Director of the University of Kentucky/University of Louisville Joint Center for the Study of Education Policy. Her most recent book, *Surviving School Micropolitics: Strategies for Administrators*, includes parent and community involvement, strategies for conflict management, and the implementation and evaluation of educational policy and reforms.

Catherine A. Lugg is Assistant Professor of Education at the Graduate School of Education, Rutgers University. Her research interests include educational politics and policy, the US religious right, and semotics. She is the author of *For God and Country: Conservatism and American School Policy* (Peter Lang, 1996) and is completing *Kitsch and Public Policy* (Garland).

Hanne B. Mawhinney is an Associate Professor and Director of Professional Development Programs in the Faculty of Education, University of Ottawa, where her work concentrates in the study of educational administration, policy and politics. Her research on accountability appears in *International Journal of Educational Research*. Other research on educational policy appears in the 1996 PEA Yearbook, *The Politcs of Education and the New Institutionalism*, which she co-edited with Robert Crowson and William Lowe Boyd. Her work is represented in *Feminist Critical Policy Analysis* (Catherine Marshall, ed.). Her research on school-community linkages, funded by the Canadian Social Sciences and Humanities Research Council, has been published in *Educational Administration Quarterly*, in the 1993 PEA Yearbook, and in *Educational Policy*. She is currently completing a chapter with Claire Smrekar on school-linked integrated services for an upcoming AERA *Handbook of Educational Administration*.

Martha McCarthy, Chancellor Professor at Indiana University, specializes in education law and policy. Previously Director of the Indiana Education Policy Center and Associate Dean of the Faculties at IU she has also been a public school teacher and central office administrator. She has served as President of the Educational Law Association and the University Council for Educational Administration and Vice President (Division A) of the American Educational Research Association. Recent books include *Continuity and Change: The Educational Leadership Professoriate* (with George Kuh) and *Public School Law: Teachers' and Students' Rights* (With Nelda Cambron-McCabe and Stephen Thomas).

Bakhyt Nadirbekkyzy was formerly a teacher and Assistant Principal at Tokish Bokin School, just outside of the capital city of Almaty, Kazakstan. Today she is an Assistant Professor of English in the Foreign Languages Department at the National Academy of Management in her native country, and spent several months in the USA on an academic exchange in 1995. Fluent in English, Kazak and Russian, she has translated several texts from English in Kazak and from Kazak into English under sponsorship of her government.

J. Anthony Riffel is Professor of Educational Administration at the University of Manitoba, where he has also served as Department Head and Associate Dean. Much of his writing has focused on issues of educational policy; his teaching has concentrated on alternative ways of organizing teacher education.

Mahna Schwager, a Senior Evaluation Associate, received her PhD in Educational Psychology and Policy from the University of California, Riverside. She has authored and co-authored several publications appearing in national and international journals and presented at state and national conferences on learning, assessment and evaluation. Recent publications include an article on teachers' perceptions on learning and assessment in the *Journal of Cognitive Education* and an article on teachers perceptions and school environments in a special assessment issue of *Education and Urban Society*. She recently received an Outstanding Paper Award from the Classroom Assessment Special Interest Group of the American Educational Research Association and, previously, a dissertation grant award from the Southwest Regional Laboratory Research Training Project.

Jean E. Treiman, an instructor at California Lutheran University, is currently finishing requirements for a PhD in Education with an emphasis in educational policy and sociology at the University of California, Riverside. Her research involves assessment reform and focuses on the varied uses of student portfolios in school work. Prior to teaching at university level, she was a classroom practitioner and site administrator. She has authored and co-authored several research articles and book chapters. Recent work includes an article on implementing new standards in teacher preparation programs published in the California Educational Research Yearbook, an evaluation report for a statewide pilot project on alternative assessment, and a research report on school district systemic reform published by the California Educational Research Cooperative. In 1994 she received a Chancellor's award for Outstanding Research Fellow and is currently President of the California Association of Colleges of Teacher Education, the state affiliate of the national association, AACTE.

James G. Ward is Professor of Educational Administration, and Professor, Institute of Government and Public Affairs, University of Illinois at Urbana-Champaign, where he is a specialist in educational policy, politics and finance. He is a past President of the American Education Finance Association and is former National Director of Research for the American Federation of Teachers. He is editor of *Who Pays for Student Diversity? Population Changes and Educational Policy* (Corwin, 1992). His recent work has focused on the application of democratic theory to education administration and policy.

Introduction and overview: Mapping shifting community relationships in children's worlds — expertise vs responsiveness

Jane Clark Lindle
University of Kentucky

The immediately preceding 1995 *Yearbook of the Politics of Education Association* focused on the new institutionalism (Crowson *et al.* 1996), which is a concept significantly linked to the theme of this, the 1996 Yearbook. The tensions between schools and families within their communities befuddle devotees of 'The American Dream', a dream of living well which honors the sanctity of both home and school as institutions and which, not surprisingly, is a broader global aspiration than the term implies. At the core of these tensions is a tattered social contract which embodies the challenges to institutionalism which were compellingly illustrated in the 1995 *Yearbook of the Politics of Education Association* (Crowson *et al.* 1996).

The current Yearbook is designed to explore more fully the confusions and demands of the pact between families, communities and schools. This volume is an exploration of the various obligations for schools as social institutions, but ultimately, our authors reveal the counter-culture nature of schooling in various international settings.

The social contract which legitimizes schooling is not merely bilateral. This multi-party bargain responds to both public and private interests in producing educated citizens or competent workers.

While families clearly represent private investment in schooling by surrendering their children to the institution, community and societal interests are not so clearly public interests. To the extent that economies are underwritten by private stakes, community interests are not necessarily vested in the greater good. To the extent that teachers are part of an entrepreneurial economic system, the social institution of schooling is run by privateers. Thus we have the conundrum of purpose in schooling.

We have a social institution contracted for societal continuity but responding to a culture sustained by private economies and nourished by individualistic values. As an institution, the school is at the nexus of social and cultural inconsistencies at the same time its contract specifies an obligation to provide both social and cultural constancy. Schools, merely by addressing their obligations, appear counter-culture to one or more of the parties to the institutional contract.

A current resurgence of political cachet in the USA for such rhetorical terms as 'family' and 'community' underscores the challenges for educators to respond to demands and social obligations in their immediate communities. Given a sustained era of educational reform, educators are reluctant to relinquish their hard-won professional discretion to respond to private and individualistic assertions by families and

0268–0939/97 $12 · 00 © 1997 Taylor & Francis Ltd.

communities. Our authors in this Yearbook provide an insight into the pressures for both expertise and responsiveness.

Mapping shifting professional and community relationships

Rich volumes of literature document erratic links between families (or communities) and schools (Blase 1987, Hollister 1979, Lightfoot 1978, Lindle 1992). These volumes speak to us of socioeconomic differences or gender-related sociocultural influences on school and family relationships. The purpose of this Yearbook is to explore the political ramifications of socioinstitutional challenges to both families and educators.

Part I is devoted to an explication of the issues surrounding professional and personal interests. Each of the three chapters draws from different intellectual traditions in mapping movement between professionals and individuals, educators and society. The map could be larger than these three representations, but this first part of the Yearbook is constrained to frame the issues for the succeeding sections. In Chapter 1, Mark Ginsberg gives us an overview of how teacher professionalism was established through increasing politicization of teacher identity and teacher unions.

David Plank's Chapter 2 is a response to the political rhetoric surrounding the term community. Plank interprets the various denotations meant by ubiquitous word, 'community.' Chapter 3 and the conclusion to Part 1 is an essay by James Ward which lays out one understanding of the political debates about schooling.

Part II shifts our attention to the front lines of professional and community relationships. These three chapters provide insight into the daily interactions characterizing the professional and personal junction. In Chapter 4, Hanne Mawhinney and Charles Kerchner pursue an ecology-of-games framework. Mawhinney and Kerchner propose to generate economic and social renewal through reinvigorating school capacity. Then, in Chapters 5 and 6, we obtain a direct view of the differing perspectives parents and professionals hold on schooling. For the parents' view in Chapter 5, Stephen Crump provides data from Australia on the tensions and trade-offs in home–school partnerships. In Chapter 6, Benjamin Levin and Anthony Riffel share Canadian data which illustrate how eduators are bereft of either analytical tools or effective responses in facing the challenges posed by changing family structures.

Part III addresses the essential issues posed by the emerging issues of democracy in the late twentieth century. Duane Covrig's Chapter 7 confronts the legacy of the eighteenth century's enlightened separation of church and state with the contemporary rejuvenation of conservative and fundamentalistic religious tenets. Covrig argues that besides families and schools, churches are the only other institution socially and culturally devoted to children's futures. Then, Martha McCarthy cites lessons from recent efforts to privatize education. In Chapter 8, McCarthy documents current trends in redefining the social contract between schools and society. She cautions about the movement from public schooling to individual contracts between schools and private interests. Chapter 9 takes us to one of the newest democratic nations, Kazakhstan. Alan DeYoung and Bakhytkul Nadirbekkyzy describe the challenges of establishing public education and empowering communities in a nation-state where imperialistic traditions and state interests historically dominated both professionals and families.

In Part IV, we conclude with two chapters which refocus our attention on the more immediate issues confronting classroom teachers and parents. Sandy Azar explains in Chapter 10 how parents and teachers view their roles in children's lives. Azar helps us recognize the generalized models teachers use in working with children. She sets these professional models in bas-relief against the particularized concerns of parents about their own children's lives. Then in Chapter 11, Jean Tremain and Mahna Schwager relive for us the disputes between teachers and parents over alternative assessment in California.

Maureen McClure draws us to a conclusion by depicting how a re-evaluation of schools' social contract with communities impacts on the social capital of communities. As we developed this book we were especially concerned with the relative isolation of schools and school personnel from the bonds and interests of communities and neighbourhoods. This isolation is increasingly apparent owing to the evolving nature of family structures as well as the intense redefinitions of national and economic structures. As boundaries devolve among nations and economic interests, schools can no longer exist as secluded institutions with specific educative tasks apart from families and communities. Therefore, with this volume we challenge the experts–school personnel–to address new relationships with the laity–parents, community leaders, churches and businesses.

References

BLASE, J. J. (1987) The politics of teaching: the teacher–parent relationship and the dynamics of diplomacy. *Journal of Teacher Educations*, **38**(2), 53–60.

CROWSON, R. L., BOYD, W. L. and MAWHINNEY, H. B. (1996) *The Politics of Education and the New Institutionalism: Reinventing the American School* (Washington, DC: Falmer Press).

HOLLISTER, C D. (1979) School bureaucratization as a response to parents' demands. *Urban Education*, **14**(2), 221–235.

LIGHTFOOT, S. L. (1978) *Worlds Apart: Relationships Between Families and Schools* (New York: Basic Books).

LINDLE, J. C. (1992) Parents and schools: public and private tensions in representations of expertise. A paper presented at the annual meeting of the American Educational Reearch Association, San Francisco.

Part 1

1.   *Professionalism or politics as a model for educators' engagement with/in communities[1]*

Mark B. Ginsburg
University of Pittsburgh

Introduction

In recent years in the USA (and other societies) we have witnessed a resurgence of activism by the religious right and other conservatives seeking to shape social policies and public institutions, including those in education. While not wanting to demonize such activity, I wish to discuss the choice of models that educators with a more secular or less conservative orientation should adopt in their efforts with/in communities to improve educational institutions and the world for children and ourselves. I will focus on whether as educators we should conceptualize and organize our work and lives in schools and communities around the notion of professionalism or politics.

For many people the answer is obvious – professionalism. In this essay, however, I will deconstruct the concepts of professionalism and politics, drawing on literature from a range of societies, in order to suggest why the answer is not so obvious. Indeed, I will argue that politics, particularly democratic politics, may be a more appropriate model for educators to adopt, at least in part, because although professionalism constitutes a form of politics, its form may be inherently undemocratic. Thus, it would be unacceptable to adopt professionalism in dealing with the perceived anti-democratic agenda of the religious right and other conservatives.

Professionalism

Despite Hall's (1983) claim that the sociological study of professions is moribund, the idea of professionalism cannot be ignored when examining contemporary societies (Macdonald and Ritzer 1988), at least where English constitutes an important language (Hughes 1966, Jackson 1970, Larson 1977). This more general statement is especially valid for educators (Pickle 1990).

The scholarly literature – as well as everyday discourse (Dingwall 1976) and the mass media – is replete with representations of what 'professionalism' means (for summaries of the literature, see Wilenski 1964, Johnson 1972, Roth 1974, Esland 1980). Not surprisingly, given a focus on different historical and social contexts as well as on different occupations, these representations, despite overlapping, vary considerably (Vollmer and Mills 1966, Jackson 1970, Johnson 1972, 1973, Klegon 1978, Ginsburg *et al.* 1980, Friedson 1983, Ginsburg 1987, Kimball 1996). Some of the traits that have been postulated to differentiate professions from other occupations (including teaching) or to characterize the elements that need to be acquired during

0268–0939/97 $12 · 00 © 1997 Taylor & Francis Ltd.

the process of professionalization include: (a) performing an essential service or task; (b) engaging in (mental versus manual) work involving a high level of expertise and judgement, thus necessitating extensive preservice education; (c) functioning based on an ideal of service; (d) operating with autonomy in the workplace; (e) having colleagues (versus non-professionals) in control of selection, training, and advancement in the field; and (f) receiving a high level of remuneration.

It is important to note that rather than being neutral concepts, 'the words "profession," "professional," "professionalization" [have until recently been] charged with laudatory meanings' (Metzger 1987: 10, see also Sykes 1989: 253). And while there are historical antecedents, it is only since the 1960s that the positive aura of professionalism has been more frequently challenged both in the literature and in everyday life. As an example, Illich (1973) refers to 'professions as a form of imperialism'.

Regardless of the valence one assigns to its meaning, professionalism should be recognized as an ideology – 'not only an image which. . .inspires collective or individual efforts, but a mystification which. . .obscures [or at least provides a partial representation of] real social structures' (Larson 1977: viii). The ideology of professionalism can be used by members of an occupational group, including educators, to maintain or acquire (1) a monopoly of the market for their 'expert' services and thus (2) obtain higher remuneration, (3) elevated social status, and (4) autonomy in their work (Hughes 1966, Vollmer and Mills 1966, Johnson 1972, Roth 1974, Dingwall 1976, Collins 1979, Esland 1980).

Professionalization, proletarianization, and the ideology of professionalism

In looking at dynamics between occupations and other groups, we also need to consider what from a Weberian perspective would be called deprofessionalization and from a Marxist perspective would be termed proletarianization. Deprofessionalization constitutes an opposite movement to professionalization through which workers' remuneration, status, and power/autonomy are diminished relative to other groups of workers as well as managers, employers, and state elites (Haug 1975, Collins 1979). Similarly, proletarianization involves a process through which the work of an occupational group is altered towards: (1) separating conception from execution of work tasks, (2) standardizing and routinizing work tasks, (3) intensifying the demands of work, and (4) reducing the costs (salaries, benefits, training, etc.) of workers (Esland 1980, Johnson 1980, Larson 1980).

The historical record in various countries illustrates that educators have experienced professionalization (e.g. Blum 1969, La Volpa 1980, Ozga and Lawn 1981, Spring 1986, Grace 1987, Jarausch 1990) as well as deprofessionalization or proletarianization (White 1981, Dove 1986, Filson 1988). Moreover, professionalization and deprofessionalization or proletarianization dynamics have affected different groups of educators differently during any given period in whichever society (Ginsburg 1991, 1995). Contrast can be noted, for instance, between teachers and administrators; between public and private school employees; among pre-school, primary school, secondary school, post-secondary school, and adult educators; and between male and female educational workers. Thus, even in the context of moves by state and economic elites to proletarianize the work of teachers, some educators may obtain increased status, power, and remuneration.

In these and other instances some groups of educators have sought to bolster their case for professionalization and against deprofessionalization or proletarianization by drawing on one or another version of the ideology of professionalism. However, the ideology of professionalism has not always been an effective tool in educators' attempt to influence their work situation. In part, this is because administrators, state elites, other occupational groups, and other citizens have employed elements from an ideology of professionalism to criticize or challenge teachers' claims and aspirations (Ozga and Lawn 1981, Filson 1988).

Professionalism in the service of elites

The fact that it is a double-edged sword might be reason enough to discard professionalism as a model for educators' engagement within communities. However, an even more compelling reason is that the extent to which educators or other occupational groups are successful in their professionalization projects by drawing on an ideology of professionalism depends not only on their rhetorical or persuasive capacity. It also depends on whether they serve the interest of economic and political elites, i.e. capital and the state, both within a particular society and internationally in colonial and neo-colonial contexts (Johnson 1973, 1980, Esland 1980, Boreham 1983, Macdonald and Ritzer 1988).

The issue here is not just that 'the process of professionalization is inextricably linked to the kind of society [or world-system] in which it takes place – to its political form, its cultural norms, and its social structure' (Vollmer and Mills 1966: 62; see also Parsons 1954). Rather the concern is that through their reliance on the ideology of professionalism, educators and other occupational groups 'have become harnessed to a much wider web of power and control in society' (Esland 1980: 213) such that 'symbiotic relations' have been established between at least some members of the professions and dominant economic and political classes (Klegon 1978: 271). In this context, although counter-hegemonic outcomes are possible (see Johnson 1980, Ginsburg 1987), it is likely that simplistically appropriating ideology of professionalism leads educators and other occupational groups to preserve the status quo and the interests of those in power. Not only might occupational groups seeking to be recognized as professions adopt racist, sexist, classist, and nativist rhetoric to exclude lower status groups from their ranks (Collins 1979, Sykes 1989, Jarausch 1990), but they might also perform their duties in ways that help preserve institutional arrangements that primarily benefit elite groups (Esland 1980, Spring 1986, Ginsburg 1995).

Professionalism as a conspiracy against the laity?

Although within some versions of the ideology of professionalism the interests of employers, clients, the general public, and 'professionals' are characterized as identical or at least in harmony, this is not necessarily the case (Roth 1974). Indeed, George Bernard Shaw's description of professions being a 'conspiracy against the laity' seems accurate, at least for those occupational groups organizing under certain versions of the ideology of professionalism. As Esland (1980: 246) discusses, a 'major characteristic of the professional mandate is that it is dependent for its justification on a somewhat negative view of the lay public'.

Adopting professionalism as a model for educators' engagement with/in communities may be inappropriate because of the undemocratic tendency within many versions of the ideology not only to distance teachers from parents, students, and other members of the community but to establish a hierarchical relation between professionals and the lay public (Pickle 1990, Zeichner 1991).

In concluding this section on professionalism, I want to clarify that by problematizing professionalism as a model for educators I am not aligning myself with the conservative attack on educators which has been associated with debates and struggles concerning educational 'reform' in recent years in a wide range of societies (see Ginsburg 1991). Instead of pushing teachers and their organizations out of educational policy making and other forms of engagement with/in communities, I encourage educators to become more involved in shaping education as well as local, national, and global communities. However, I am proposing that rather than pursuing an isolated and isolating politics of professionalism, educators develop a particular form of democratic politics in which educators work energetically and effectively in relation to parents, other workers, and citizens.

Politics

For some scholars, such as Gramsci (1971: 62), 'the meaning of human nature is. . .at its very core, "political".' However, for many people in various societies 'politics' has a negative connotation (see Ginsburg 1995). Indeed, the noun 'politics' and the adjective 'political' seem increasingly to be employed in a pejorative manner. Educators have also shunned − or at least sought to distance the public's perception of themselves from − politics (Lee 1987, Sautman 1991), even while efforts to discourage educators from being 'political' have been anything but neutral (Blum 1969, Lawn 1985, Spring 1986).

Politics, power-over, and power-with

Educators' concerns derive at least partly from the assumption that domination (dominating or being dominated) is the only, or necessary, type of relationship involved in politics. This assumption is evidenced, for instance, when prospective educators in Mexico say that they want to avoid engaging in political activity because it would involve them with people who are primarily concerned with controlling others or accumulating material and symbolic resources at the expense of others (Ginsburg and Tidwell 1990).

I agree that at its core politics is intimately linked to power (see Mills 1956, Lasswell 1977, Foucault 1980), just as power is a central element of professionalism as well. Politics is concerned with the control of the means of producing, reproducing, consuming, and accumulating material and symbolic resources (Dove 1986). To locate power relations at the heart of politics, however, is not tantamount to equating politics with dominant–subordinate relations. I differ, therefore, with John Stuart Mill (1861: 39) when he states that there are only two 'inclinations. . .one the desire to exercise power over others; the other. . .to [not] have power exercised over themselves'. That is, power over is only one aspect of power, the other aspect is power with. Both aspects of power exist in dialectical relationshp to each other at the core of politics, although one aspect may be more clearly evidenced in any given situation.

'Power over' is the aspect of power that has been emphasized more often by theorists and perhaps by political actors. It involves the capacity to get people to act, to not act, or to not even consider acting in ways that are contrary to their interests (Lukes 1974). In contrast, according to Kreisberg:

> Power with is manifest in relationships of co-agency. These relationships are characterised by people finding ways to satisfy their desires and to fulfil their interests without imposing on one another. The relationship of co-agency is one in which there is equality: situations in which individuals and groups fulfil their desire by acting together. It is jointly developing capacity. (1992: 85)

While the notion of power over implies that power 'is a scarce resource to be coveted, hoarded, and used in one's own interest [so that] there are winners and losers', the idea of power with characterizes power as 'an expanding renewable resource available through shared endeavours, dialogue, and co-operation' (Kreisberg 1992: 32, 63).

Politics and public/private spheres

Another questionable assumption buttressing the argument that educators are or should be 'apolitical' is that personal and political matters or private and public sphere activity can be clearly separated. Educators are not (or should not be) considered to be political because many of them, especially women, are not (or should not be) actively or visibly involved in 'public sphere' activity, such as participation in union/ professional organizations, 'political' parties, and other community-based citizen groups and movements. The implicit assumption here is that the personal-level interactions educators have with students, colleagues, educational authorities in the 'private sphere' of classrooms and schools are excluded from the political realm (Corr and Jamieson 1990).

I do not accept such a narrow definition of the concept of political; rather in line with feminist ideas I postulate that: (1) the personal is political and the political is personal and (2) public and private are not separate spheres. What educators do in the 'private spheres' of classrooms, laboratories, libraries, meeting rooms, and offices is a form of political action as is 'public sphere' participation or non-participation in picket lines, demonstrations, lobbying, voting, running for office, and (armed or unarmed) revolutionary or anti-colonial struggle. The terms, politics and political, are not limited to considerations of the state, governments, parties, constitutions, and voting (Corr and Jamieson 1990). 'Politics is how you live your life, not whom you vote for' (Nichols 1977: 183). All aspects of human experience have a political dimension.

Educators and politics

Educators neither operate in a political vacuum nor are they neutral (Lawn 1985). What educators do occurs in a context of power relations and distributions of symbolic and material resources; as well, educators' action (or inaction) has political implications for themselves and others. Thus educators are political actors regardless of whether they are active or passive; autonomous or heteronomous *vis-à-vis* other groups; conservative or change oriented; seeking individual, occupational group, or larger collectivities' goals; and/or serving dominant group, subordinate group, or, more generally, human interests.

The question for educators, therefore, is not the Shakespearean question 'to be or not to be' political, but rather what kind of politics to pursue – through what kinds of processes and in whose interests. The answer I propose for educators' consideration is 'democratic' politics.

Democracy and democratic politics

While serious concerns have been expressed about the vitality of institutions in societies which have for many years been characterized as 'democracies' (Elshtain 1994, Lasch 1994), at the same time there appears to be 'universal enthusiasm for democracy' by social theorists as well as other people residing in an increasing number of countries around the world (Giddens 1994: 104). Diamond and Plattner (1993) refer to this latter development as a 'global resurgence of democracy'.

Since democracy has many meanings, I will try to clarify the conceptualization of democracy that I bring to this discussion. Following Highland (1995), I conceive of a power structure or set of social relations as democratic to the extent that 'all those who are subject to the decisions have equal effective rights in the determination of decisions to which they are subject' (p. 67). 'Equal effective rights' entail more than individuals (or groups) having procedural entitlements, that is, the right (directly) to vote to determine decisions or (indirectly) to elect those who vote to determine decisions. Rather having equal effective rights necessitates 'both procedural entitlements to participate in a decision-making process and adequate access to a wide range of [material and symbolic] resources that would enable a person to utilise her or his procedural entitlements' (Highland 1995: 2). Thus, democracy is accomplished through the equalization of material and symbolic resources – or at least the distribution of such resources to enable equal effective rights – and by de-emphasizing power-over and stressing power-with relations (Highland 1995: 44–45). This conception of democracy also has affinities with what Giddens (1994: 113) calls 'dialogic democracy' in that decisions are arrived at via 'open and uncoerced discussion' as well as through negotiation among equally situated participants.

Conclusion

While suggesting dialogic democratic politics or what Aronowitz (1994) terms 'radical democracy' as a model for educators' engagement with/in communities, I do not do so naively. From Giddens (1994: 131) I understand that 'democratic dialogic spaces'...must in some way be filled. These are spaces which can be engaged with dialogically, invoking mechanisms of active trust – but which can also be occupied by fundamentalism. And in line with Epstein's (1994: 108) concerns about Aronowitz's (1994) conception of 'radical democracy', I recognize that 'popular participation does not always produce the politics we would like'. For example, in the context of debates and decision making regarding the reform of schools, dialogic or radical democracy poses critical challenges for those who have progressive visions for how schools and society should be organized to serve the interests of our children and ourselves. As Zeichner observes:

In these times of conservative resurgence, supporting a greater role for communities in running their schools makes schools more vulnerable to the wishes and desires of those who seek to force antidemocratic beliefs onto the public schools. . .repressing particular points of view or discriminating against certain groups of people. (1991: 364, 370)

Distates for the agenda of the 'religious right' or other conservatives might lead us to want to close down democratic dialogic spaces, notably by asserting the sole legitimacy of 'professional' experts to make decisions about education and society. I hope, instead, that, as educators, we will join with others in the context of power-with relations to forge spaces in which democracy obtains, not only procedurally but also substantively. If we really were to move toward substantive democracy (i.e. providing all people with the material and symbolic resources to insure equal effective rights), I believe that the appeal to religious and other conservative ideologies (the simple answers to problems in inequality and the scape-goating of those who really are not the cause of such problems) will be considerably diminished. Regardless, I find it untenable to counter threats to democracy by asserting professionals' privilege to decide what is best for our children.

Note

1. This is a revised and abridged version of a paper prepared as the keynote address at the Hong Kong Educational Research Association's 12th conference, Hong Kong, 11–12 November 1995. Chapter to be included in Jane Clark Lindle and Maureen McClure (eds) (1996/97) *Shifting Professional and Community Relationships in Children's Worlds: Expertise vs. Responsibility* (New York: Falmer).

References

ARONOWITZ, S. (1994) Radical democracy: the situation of the left in the United States. *Socialist Review,* **23**(3), 5–79.

BLUM, A. (ed.) (1969) *Teacher Unions And Associations* (Urban, IL: University of Illinois Press).

BOREHAM, P. (1983) Indetermination: professional knowledge, organization and control. *Socioloical Review,* **31**, 693–718.

COLLINS, R. (1979) The politics of professions. In *The Credential Society: A Historical Sociology Of Education And Stratification* (New York: Academic Press), 131–181.

CORR, H. and JAMIESON, L. (1990) *Politics of Everyday Life: Continuity And Change In Work And The Family* (London: Macmillan).

DIAMOND, L. and PLATTNER, M. (1993) *The Global Resurgence Of Democracy* (Baltimore, MD: Johns Hopkins Press).

DINGWALL, R. (1976) Accomplishing profession. *Sociological Review,* **24**, 331–349.

DOVE, L. (1986) *Teachers In Politics In Developing Countries* (London: Croom Helm).

ELSHTAIN, J. B. (1994) *Democracy On Trial* (New York: Basic Books).

EPSTEIN, B. (1994) Response to Aronowitz's 'situation of the left in the United States'. *Socialist Review,* **23**(3), 107–112.

ESLAND, G. (1980) Professions and professionalism. In G. Esland and G. Salaman (eds), *The Politics Of Work And Occupations* (Milton Keynes, England: Open University Press), 213–250.

FILSON, G. (1988) Ontario teachers' deprofessionalisation and proletarianisation. *Comparative Education Review,* **32**, 298–317.

FOUCAULT, M. (1980) *Power/Knowledge* (New York: Pantheon).

FREIDSON, E. (1983) The theory of the professions: the state of the art. In R. Dingwall and P. Lewis (eds), *The Sociology Of The Professions* (New York: St. Martin's), 19–37.

GIDDENS, A. (1994) *Beyond Left And Right: The Future Of Radical Politics* (Stanford, CA: Stanford University Press).

GINSBURG, M. (1987) Reproduction, contradiction and conceptions of professionalism: the case of preservice teachers. In T. Popkewitz (ed.), *Critical Studies In Teacher Education* (New York: Falmer) 86–129.

GINSBURG, M. (ed.) (1991) *Understanding Educational Reform In Global Context* (New York: Garland).

GINSBURG, M. (ed.) (1995) *The Politics Of Educators Work And Lives* (New York: Garland).

GINSBURG, M., MEYENN, R. and MILLER, M. (1980) Teachers conceptions of professionalism and trades unionism: an ideological analysis. In P. Woods (ed.), *Teacher Strategies* (London: Croom Helm), 178–212.

GINSBURG, M. and TIDWELL, M. (1990) Political socialisation of prospective educators in Mexico. *New Education,* **12**, 70–82.

GRACE, G. (1987) Teachers and the state in Britain. In M. Lawn and G. Grace Teachers (eds), *The Culture And Politics Of Work* (Lewes: Falmer), 193–228.

GRAMSCI, A. (1971) *Selections From Prison Notebooks* (New York: International Publishers).

HALL, R. (1983) Theoretical trends in the sociology of occupations. *Sociological Quarterly*, **24**, 5–23.

HAUG, M. (1975) The deprofessionalisation of everyone? *Sociological Focus*, **8**, 197–213.

HIGHLAND, J. (1995) *Democratic Theory: The Philosophical Foundations* (Manchester: Manchester University Press).

HUGHES, E. (1966) The social significance of professionalization. In H. Vollmer and D. Mills (eds), *Professionalization* (Englewood Cliffs, NJ: Prentice-Hall), 64–70.

ILLICH, I. (1973) The professions as a form of imperialism. *New Society*, **25**, 633–635.

JACKSON, J. (ed.) (1970) *Professions And Professionalization* (London: Cambridge University Press).

JARAUSCH, K. (1990) *The Unfree Professions: German Lawyers, Teachers, And Engineers, 1900–1950* (New York: Oxford University Press).

JOHNSON, T. (1972) *Professions And Power* (London: Macmillan).

JOHNSON, T. (1973) Imperialism and the professions: notes on the development of professional occupations in Britain's colonies and the new states. *Sociological Review*, **20**, 281–309.

JOHNSON, T. (1980) Work and power. In G. Esland and G. Salaman (eds), *The Politics Of Work And Occupations* (Milton Keynes, England: Open University Press), 335–371.

KIMBALL, B. (1996) *The True Professional Ideal In America: A History* (Lanham, MD: Roman & Littlefield).

KLEGON, D. (1978) The sociology of professions: an emerging perspective. *Sociology of Work and Occupations*, **5**(3), 259–280.

KREISBERG, S. (1992) *Transforming Power: Domination, Empowerment, And Education* (Albany, NY: State University of New York Press).

LARSON, M. (1977) *The Rise Of Professionalism* (Berkeley, CA: University of California Press).

LARSON, M. (1980) Proletarianisan of educated labour. *Theory and Society*, **9**(1), 131–175.

LASCH, C. (1994) *The Revolt Of The Elites And The Betrayal Of Democracy* (New York: W. W. Norton).

LASSWELL, H. D. (1977) *Howard D. Lasswell on Political Sociology* (Chicago: University of Chicago Press).

LAWN, M. (ed.) (1985) *The Politics Of Teacher Unionism* (London: Croom Helm).

LaVOLPA, A. (1980) *Prussian School Teachers: Profession And Office* (Chapel Hill, NC: University of North Carolina Press).

LEE, J. (1987) Pride and prejudice: teachers, class and an innercity infants school. In M. Lawn and G. Grace (eds), *Teachers: The Culture And Politics Of Work* (London: Falmer), 90–116.

LORTIE, D. (1975) *School Teacher: A Sociological Analysis* (Chicago, IL: University of Chicago Press).

LUKES, S. (1974) *Power: A Radical View* (London: British Sociological Association).

MACDONALD, K. and RITZER, G. (1988) The sociology of professions: dead or alive? *Work and Occupations*, **15**(3), 251–272.

METZGER, W. (1987) A spectre is haunting American scholars: the spectre of 'professionalism'. *Educational Researcher*, 10–19.

MILL, J. S. (1861) *Considerations On Representative Government* (London: Liberal Arts Library).

MILLS, C. W. (1956) *The Power Elite* (New York: Oxford University Press).

NICHOLS, R. L. (1977) Rebels, beginners, and buffoons: politics as action. In T. Ball (ed.), *Political Theory And Praxis* (Minneapolis, University of Minnesota Press), 159–169.

OZGA, J. and LAWN, M. (1981) *Teachers, Professionalism And Class* (London: Falmer).

PARSONS, T. (1954) The professions and social structure. In *Essays In Sociological Theory* (New York: Free Press), 34–49.

PICKLE, J. (1990) Toward a reconstruction of teacher professionalism. *Educational Foundations*, **4**(2), 73–87.

ROTH, J. (1974) Professionalism: the sociologist's decoy. *Sociology of Work and Occupations*, **1**(1), 6–23.

SAUTMAN, B. (1991) Politicisation, hyperpoliticization, and depoliticization of Chinese education. *Comparative Education Review*, **35**, 669–689.

SPRING, J. (1986) *The American School, 1642–1985* (New York: Longman).

SYKES, G. (1989) Teaching and professionalism: a cautionary perspective. In L. Weis, P. Altbach, G. Kelly and H. Petrie (eds), *Crisis In Teaching: Perspectives On Current Reforms* (Albany, NY: State University of New York Press), 253–273.

VOLLMER, H. and MILLS, D. (1966) *Professionalization* (Englewood Cliffs, NJ: Prentice-Hall).

WHITE, G. (1981) *Party And Professionals: The Political Role Of Teachers In Contemporary China* (New York: M. E. Sharpe).

WILENSKI, H. (1964) The professionalization of everyone? *American Sociological Review*, **52**(2), 137–158.

ZEICHNER, K. (1991) Contradictions and tensions in the professionalization of teaching and the democratization of schools. *Teachers College Record*, **92**(3), 364–379.

2.   *Dreams of community*

David N. Plank
Michigan State University

When I use a word, Humpty Dumpty said, in a rather scornful tone, it means just what I choose it to mean – neither more nor less. (Lewis Carol)

Introduction

Community is surely one of the most frequently used and abused words in educational policy literature. Analysts from all points on the political spectrum affirm the virtue and value of communities as an essential source of support for schools and as the guarantors of accountability in the educational system. Educators are enjoined from all sides to work in closer harmony with the community in order to fit their practice to local needs and better serve their students. Shifting a greater share of responsibility to the community is adduced as the solution to a host of problems, both in the USA and abroad.

Community is a universally popular term for educational policy becaue it encompasses many different meanings; all can agree that closer ties to the community are a good thing, as long as the term remains undefined. This apparent consensus quickly breaks down, however, in the face of inevitable disagreements about the character and size of the relevant community in particular contexts.

In this essay I seek to bring some clarity to current policy discussions by exploring some of the many meanings encompassed in the term community. In the following section I identify several of the unexamined ambiguities and oppositions encountered in recent scholarly writing about the importance of community for educational policy. In the third section I present a partial survey of the types of communities that educators might actually encounter as they venture out to look for community linkages or community support. In the final section I discuss the implications of the preceding analysis for current debates on educational reform. I conclude that affirmations of community in contemporary policy debates may often be damaging rather than helpful, for two main reasons. First, the community that is commonly invoked by policy analysts does not exist, either because it has vanished forever or because it remains to be created. Second, the community that exists in fact is often very different from the one imagined by analysts. Shifting power and responsibility to the community may therefore have unexpected and pernicious consequences.

0268–0939/97 $12 · 00 © 1997 Taylor & Francis Ltd.

Questing after community

The extravagance of meaning associated with the term community is apparent in a partial list of the qualifiers that may precede it in common usage. Among dozens of others, these include academic, African-American, beachfront, business, European, gay, Hispanic, human, international, Muslim, parent, policy, school, traditional, virtual and working class. According to Plant (1978: 80), the term may be used to refer to: 'locality; interest group; a system of solidarity; a group with a sense of mutual significance; a group characterized by moral agreement, shared beliefs, shared authority, or ethnic integrity; a group marked by historical continuity and shared traditions; a group in which members meet in some kind of total fashion as opposed to meeting as members of certain roles, functions, or occupational groups; and finally, occupational, functional, or partial communities'. The variety and mutual incompatibility of these definitions led A. H. Halsey (quoted in Plant 1978: 79) to conclude that community has 'so many meanings as to be meaningless'.

The term must nevertheless rank high on the all-time hit parade for frequency of usage in educational policy analyses. In a recent paean to the 'local school' for example, Hill, Guthrie, and Pierce (1996: 56) assert that public schools must revive 'a personal bond of reciprocity, a sense of mutual reliance. . .between the school and the broader community'. Among its policy proposals for post-apartheid education in South Africa, the African National Congress (1994: 61) calls for 'structures of institutional governance which reflect the interests of all stakeholders and the broader community served by the institution'. In an analysis of the educational obstacles facing African-American youth in US cities, Alston (1993: 125) affirms that the lives 'of these children depend on their communities' capacities to be self-assertive, radical, tenacious, and willing to continue debate'. According to the World Bank (1995: 126), 'educational quality can increase [in developing countries] when schools are able to use instructional inputs according to local school and community conditions and when they are accountable to parents and communities'. It is apparent that all of these authors regard 'the community' favourably, as an important and welcome actor in the educational policy arena. It is equally apparent that they each mean quite different things by the term, and that they would prescribe very different policies in consequence.

As educators seek to engage with communities, some clarity as to what kind of community they are looking for and what kind they expect to find is likely to be helpful. It will also be helpful to recognize at the outset that differing definitions of community summon forth deep and possible irreconcilable disagreements, rooted in competing ideologies and values. Serious considerations of the ambiguities and oppositions that give rise to these disagreements is essential to an understanding of the policy dilemmas we now face in the educational system.

One fundamental question is whether the school community is to be defined primarily in terms of geographical boundaries, or in terms of one or more dimensions of social affinity. Assigning priority to geography, as has been traditional in US public schools and school districts, fosters pluralism and inclusion at the risk of attenuated social and value coherence. Assigning priority to social bonds, as in parochial or charter schools, builds upon existing stocks of 'social capital' at the risk of permitting or encouraging particularism and exclusion. Variations in the character of communities often intersect with variations in size. Small voluntary communities (e.g. ethnic neighbourhoods, Christian schools) are likely to be closely-knit and rich in 'social capital', but at least potentially subversive of a common civic culture. Large statutorily defined communities (e.g. New York's 'community school districts') are likely to reflect the value conflicts and policy dilemmas of the broader society.

A related issue has to with the ontology of communities. There is an emergent consensus that 'social capital' is in increasingly short supply, and that support for institutions that will foster the construction or reconstruction of communities is urgently needed (Putnam 1995). The ramifications of this apparent agreement nevertheless sharply divide conservatives and progressives. The question, put simply, is whether strengthening communities requires the restoration of hierarchical order, cultural traditions, and social discipline, or the construction of new institutions based on equity, inclusion, and democratic participation (Cohen 1976, Plant 1978). From the conservative perspective, our present crisis may be seen as the consequence of a fall away from the certainties and solidarities of the past, which were deeply rooted in a received tradition (Bloom 1987, Bennett 1992). From a progressive perspective, the inequities and oppressions concealed in traditional institutions (including the family and the school) must be exposed and undone before a truly just and democratic community can be established (Marshall 1993, Dewey 1994).

Moreover, as Putnam's work on Italy makes clear, 'social capital' like other forms of capital yields its returns in kind. Those who have lots can acquire more with relatively little effort; those with little or none are hard-pressed to accumulate any in the daily struggle of all against all (Putnam 1993: 169). Reposing our faith in the intrinsic strength and virtue of communities is consequently likely to benefit those with access to lots of social capital, while it may in fact do harm to those with less, thus exacerbating social and civic inequalities.

The questions raised by these issues are easier to evade than to answer. It is comforting to think that geographical and social boundaries naturally coincide, or can be made to coincide, but in fact they need not, and often do not. It is comforting to think that communities rich in social capital are all around us, simply awaiting the call to renewed social responsibility, but in many places they are not, and assigning large public responsibilities to communities poor in social capital may make them worse rather than better off. It is comforting to think that disagreements over core values can be reconciled, but in fact these conflicts and the dilemmas they entail are a permanent feature of our political landscape (Plank and Boyd 1994). Implicit or explicit choices about the communities with whom educators engage thus address matters of profound consequence. Simply affirming the importance of community, and hoping that the features we dislike will vanish while those we like remain may well deepen rather than ameliorate the educational crisis in wich we find ourselves.

From Tocqueville to Tiebout

As Plant (1978) and others have pointed out, there are nearly as many kinds of communities as there are authors to talk about them. Any typology is therefore bound to be arbitrary and partial, but it may nevertheless be useful to suggest one possible way of thinking systematically about four types of community that are especially relevant to educators seeking to build connections with institutions outside their schools.

Autochthonous communities

These are the communities most often invoked in political rhetoric and educational policy analysis. They are *gemeinschaft* communities, bound together by common interest and mutual concern. Examples include the self-governing and self-reliant New England townships described by Tocqueville, the Italian 'civic communities' celebrated by Robert Putnam, the small towns (such as Hope, Arkansas or Russell, Kansas) that are such an asset to candidates in US presidential elections, and the 'traditional communities' in Africa and Asia that are expected to carry an increasing share of the responsibility for providing education and other social services (Tocqueville 1945, Putname 1993, World Bank 1995).

Autochthonous communities are distant in space or time or both from the *gesellschaft* world inhabited by most politicians and scholars, which enhances both their romantic allure and their mythic strength and resilience. One obvious question to ask with respect to autochthonous communities is how many such communities remain available to policy makers who wish to shift responsibilities to them. Generations of social scientists have celebrated or lamented their decline, though some (e.g. Iannaccone and Lutz 1995: 50) assert that they remain intact (or at least latent) in rural areas and 'ethnic enclaves' in large cities, waiting to be called back to life and potency by the restoration of their traditional status and powers. A second question is whether the traditionally hierarchical social structures of autochthonous communities can be reconciled to the post-industrial, multicultural world that most professional educators now inhabit.

Atavistic communities

Attempts to restore the solidarity and security of autochthonous communities are often rooted in atavistic impulses, as David Post (1992) has illustrated in his brilliant article on the curriculum wars in a small California town. In Joshua Gap, political opposition to a new 'multicultural' curriculum arose not among the long-time residents of the town, but rather among those who had recently moved in. According to Post, the latter had come to Joshua Gap in search of an idealized community removed from the conflicts and anxieties of the cities and suburbs they had left behind, and they were militant in their zeal to protect their new community from the (further) intrusions of outsiders. Autochthonous residents proved in contrast to be far more tolerant.

Elsewhere, the deterioration of the nation-sate has been accompanied by the exploitation of primordial loyalties for political gain, and by the resurgence or emergence of communities defined by language, religion, or ethnic identity (Guehenno 1995). To build a social infrastructure (or at least create the illusion) of common interest and mutual concern atavistic communities often rely on identity politics, exclusion, and intolerance as strategies for building or maintaining boundaries and enforcing compliance with community norms. For example, Hindu and Afrikaaner nationalisms represents efforts to protect or create communal traditions and community institutions based on exclusion and internal coercion. Devolving educational responsibilities to such communities may be an effective strategy for shifting costs out of the national budget, but it may in many cases be accomplished at the cost of fostering atavistic conflict in the local competition for power and resources.

Ascribed communities

The mirror image of atavistic communities is ascribed communities, which are created only partly by the deliberate choices of their members, but also by their members' exclusion from a broader national community. Common interest and mutual concern are ascribed to these communities, or asserted by aspiring community leaders, whether or not these in fact exist. For example, D'Souza's (1995) assertion that the 'black community' bears a special responsibility for looking after its less fortunate members is aimed mainly at absolution for whites, and only secondarily at improving the situation of African-Americans. Black nationalist affirmations of similar views are on the one hand a realistic response to the grim reality that whites are desperate to rid themselves of responsibility for black disadvantage. On the other hand, however, they also represent a strategy for maintaining group cohesion and facilitating political control within a specific constituency. According to Maynard (1970: 111): 'According to the blacks' view of the world, it has become necessary to take over responsibility for their own education and that of their children, partly because of the hostility they divine in white systems, but also because of their new self-involvement and, thus, their rush to self-discovery'.

Educational policies that affirm the integrity of ascribed communities by devolving authority to them may serve to enhance the dignity and autonomy of otherwise disadvantaged groups against the opposition of those in power (Levin 1970). They may simultaneously undermine the claims of common citizenship, however, and thus serve to entrench the caste boundaries that created the initial disadvantage (Fein 1970).

Atomized communities

A final set of communities is defined in part by geography, but more importantly by affinities of social class and preference. In many part of the USA citizens 'shop' for communities as they shop for the other attributes of a preferred lifestyle, moving freely from one to the next as they seek the best attainable combination of public services, tax rates, and housing quality (Tiebout 1956). The key attribute of atomized communities is thus mobility: residents dissatisfied with the package of amenities available in one community simply move to another better suited to their preferences. Citizens' loyalties to their present community are entirely contingent, and minimally reliant on bonds of common interest or mutual concern. Atomized communities consequently display little of the exclusionary fervour of atavistic communities, and almost none of the social solidarity of autochthonous communities.

The social geography of US cities is increasingly organized along these lines, with residents segregated into housing tracts developed to suit the preferences of narrowly specified segments of the housing market or abandoned to those who lack other choices (Katznelson and Weir 1985: 219). The analogy between citizens' current freedom to choose their communities and the proposed extension of their right to choose their schools is straightforward, and not especially reassuring to those who seek to build stronger communities around schools of choice.

Conjuring up community

Glendower: I can call spirits from the vasty deep.
Hotspur: Why, so can I, or so can any man, But will they come when you do call for them? (Shakespeare)

There is widespread agreement that stronger communities must be a central element in any successful strategy for addressing a variety of social ills, from rising crime to stagnant education to declining political participation. This agreement encompasses an acknowledgement that communities and community institutions are less robust than they need to be if they are to play the leading role assigned to them, and that they are consequently in need of revitalization.

Efforts to move beyond rhetorical affirmation to public action reveal profound disagreements between conservatives and progressives about how communities are to be strengthened, however. The former argue that communities were stronger in the past than they are today, that the massive growth and increased intrusiveness of the state in the past several decades has weakened community institutions, and that the restoring of communities therefore requires the diminution of state and especially federal power and the devolution of a wide array of public responsibilities back to the local level (Bennett 1992). The latter argue that the traditional communities glorified by conservatives were commonly exclusive, parochial, and oppressive to many of their members, including women and members of racial and linguistic minorities. They therefore argue that the destruction of traditional hierarchies is an essential prelude to the construction of more equitable and authentic communities in the future, and that the state (including the public schools) has an important role to play in building or rebuilding these new communities (Hochschild 1984, Guttman 1987, Dewey 1994).

A number of cheerful and probably unwarranted assumptions underlie both of these views. Common to both camps is the assumption that the communities that they desire can be easily called forth, while those of which they disapprove can be as easily dispensed with. Among conservatives, for example, the key assumption is that vital and resilient autochthonous communities remain widely available to policy makers, to be restored to power and responsibility as the powers of federal and state governments are reduced. Among progressives the analogous assumption holds that many communities have been shattered or profoundly weakened, but that they can nevertheless be summoned into service when needed to assume major political and administrative responsibilities or to enforce accountability on other levels of government. Both groups agree, however, that communities – once restored to their rightful place in the political order – will exemplify norms and values that correspond closely to the norms and values of those who are doing the calling.

Recent instances in which educational policy initiatives have relied heavily on the availability of communities as political resources include school governance reforms in Chicago and the myriad proposals and projects that have lately been put forward under the banner of 'coordinated children's services'. In both cases policy makers have reached out to the community with some confidence that this was a good idea, but without a strong prior sense of what they would find.

Early evidence showed that 'strong democracy' had emerged in about one-third of Chicago schools, and something less than strong democracy (adversarial politics, maintenance politics, consolidated principal power) in the other two thirds (CCSR 1993: 7–8). How these other schools were to be introduced to or prepared for 'strong democracy' was never made clear; the implicit assumption appears to have been that communities handed responsibility for governing and managing local schools would simply step up and organize themselves. More recent evidence shows a dramatic decline in the number of candidates for school councils and in the rate of participation in council elections (Wong *et al.* 1995); assigning important taks to community institutions turns out to be an insufficiently powerful charm to conjure these institutions into being.

Experience has been similar in the case of 'co-ordinated children's services', in which reformers typically look forward to building 'better' communities whose norms and values will correspond more closely to the norms and values of the professionals who serve them (Crowson and Boyd 1993, Adler 1994: 10, Mawhinney 1994: 42). Reaching out to the community where no community exists may well produce more comprehensive and more powerful networks of professionals, but under many circumstances it will not and perhaps cannot produce a true partnership with constituents.

Many of the issues raised by the Chicago school reforms and 'co-ordinated children's services' are issues of power, which raise the question of the extent to which professional educators are prepared to cede power and authority to parents and lay governors, especially when community values and preferences conflict with deeply held professional norms (Hess 1993: 94). For example, when communities demand that the local school teach creationism, or organize separate programmes for African-American males, on what basis are teachers prepared to go along, or to refuse? It is not enough to assume that the community's values must or will correspond to the values of those who seek to 'care for' or 'empower' them.

It is worth noting in this connection that, despite the intense rhetorical enthusiasm for communities in current policy debates, a variety of recent policy initiatives and structural changes in the public school system have undermined rather than strengthened the role of communities in educational governance. Notable examples include state and national standards, enforced by testing and backed up with the threat of state take-overs; and the move to student-based funding, which greatly strengthens the 'exit' capabilities of parents and correspondingly weakens the claims of community institutions upon their putative members.

Dreams of community

The central role assigned to communities in recent writing on educational policy is not misplaced; restoring the connection between schools and those they nominally serve is a task of the utmost importance. Shifting power and resources to communities without careful consideration of what is at stake may have damaging consequences, however, including increased fragmentation and inequality along racial, ethnic, and class lines; further abdication of the responsibilities and obligations of common citizenship; and accelerated deterioration in many parts of the public school system. Finding ways to engage citizens more deeply in the governance of their schools without succumbing to these centrifugal forces is bound to be a profoundly difficult challenge. Giving some thought to its difficulty may increase the likelihood that it will be successfully met.

References

ADLER, L. (1994) Introduction and overview, in L. Adler and S. Gardner (eds), *The Politics Of Linking Schools And Social Services* (London: Falmer Press), 33–47.

AFRICAN NATIONAL CONGRESS (1994) *The Reconstruction And Development Programme* (Johannesburg: Umanyano Publications).

ALSTON, K. (1993) Community politics and the education of African American males: whose life is it anyway?, In C. Marshall (ed.), *The New Politics Of Race And Gender* (London: Falmer Press), 107–116.

BENNETT, W. (1992) *The De-Valuing Of America. The Fight For Our Culture And Our Children* (New York: Simon & Schuster).

BLOOM, A. (1987) *The Closing Of The American Mind* (New York: Simon & Schuster).

COHEN, D. K. (1976) Loss as a theme in social policy. *Harvard Educational Review,* 46(4), 553–571.

CONSORTIUM ON CHICAGO SCHOOL RESEARCH (1993) *A View From The Schools: The State Of Reform In Chicago* (Chicago, IL: Author).

CROWSON, R. L. and BOYD, W. L. (1993) Cooridnated services for children: designing arks for storms and seas unknown. *American Journal of Education,* 101(2), 140–179.

DEWEY, J. (1994) The great community. In M. Daly (ed.), *Communitarianism: A New Public Ethnic* (Belmont, CA: Wadsworth), 154–165.

D'SOUZA, D. (1995) *The End Of Racism: Principles For A Multiracial Society* (New York: Free Press).

FEIN. L. J. (1970) Community schools and social theory: the limits of universalism, in H. M. Levin (ed.), *Community Control of Schools* (Washington: Brookings Institution), 76–99.

GUEHENNO, J. M. (1995) *The End of the Nation-State* (Minneapolis, MN: University of Minnesota Press).

GUTTMAN, A. (1987) *Democratic Education* (Princeton, NJ: Princeton University Press).

HESS, G. A., JR (1993) Race and the liberal perspective in Chicago school reform, in C. Marshall (ed.), *The New Politics Of Race And Gender* (London: Falmer Press), 85–96.

HILL, P., GUTHRIE, J. W. and PIERCE, L. (1996) Whatever happened to the local school? *Education Week,* 56, 33.

HOCHSCHILD, J. L. (1984) *The New American Dilemma: Liberal Democracy And School Desegregation* (New Haven: Yale University Press).

IANNACCONE, L. and LUTZ, F. W. (1995) The crucible of democracy: the local arena, in J. D. Scribner and D. H. Layton (eds), *The Study of Educational Politics* (London: Falmer Press), 39–52.

KATZNELSON, I. and WEIR, M. (1985) *Schooling For All: Class, Race, And The Decline Of The Democratic Ideal* (New York: Basic Books).

LEVIN, HENRY M. (1970) *Community Control of Schools* (Washington: Brookings Institution).

MARSHALL, C. (1993) *The New Politics of Race and Gender* (London: Falmer).

MAWHINNEY, HANNE B. (1994) Discovering shared values: ecological models to support interagency collaboration, in L. Adler and S. Gardner (eds), *The Politics Of Linking Schools And Social Service* (London: Falmer Press), 33–47.

MAYNARD, R. C. (1970) Black nationalism and community schools, in H. M. Levin (ed.), *Community Control Of Schools* (Washington: Brookings Institution), 100–111.

PLANK, D. N. and BOYD, W. L. (1994) Anti-politics, institutional choice, and educational policy: the fight from democracy. *American Educational Research Journal,* 31(2), 263–281.

PLANT, R. (1978) Community: concept, conception, and ideology, *Politics and Society,* 8(1), 49–78.

POST, D. (1992) Through Joshua Gap: curricular control and the constructed community. *Teachers College Record,* 93, 673–696.

PUTNAM, R. D. (1993) *Making Democracy Work: Civic Traditions in Modern Italy* (Princeton, NJ: Princeton University Press).

PUTNAM, R. D. (1995) The prosperous community: social capital and public life, in W. D. Burnham (ed.), *The American Prospect Reader in American Politics* (Chatham, NJ: Chatham House), 61–72.

TIEBOUT, C. M. (1956) The pure theory of local expenditure. *Journal of Political Economy,* 64, 416–424.

TOCQUEVILLE, ALEXIS DE (1945) *Democracy in America,* Vol. 1 (New York: Vintage Books).

WONG, K. K. DREEBEN, R., LYNN, L., MEYER, R. and SUNDERMAN, G. (1995) *System-Wide Governance In The Chicago Public Schools: Findings And Recommendations For Institutional Redesign* (Processed).

WORLD BANK (1995) *Priorities And Strategies For Education* (Washington: IBRD).

3.   *Theories of politics and the legitimacy of public schools in a democratic state*

James G. Ward
University of Illinois at Urbana-Champaign

The paradox of the debates over public schools

The current debates over public education in the USA are replete with paradoxes. There is a cacophony of opinion and contradictory statements about the condition of the US public school. For example, while some commentators argue that the US public schools are utter failures in preparing students to meet the needs of an information-based, global economy, others document how public schools may be doing a better job than ever (Berliner and Biddle 1995, Bracey 1996). Also, we hear that schools are working hard to teach to the needs and values of a pluralistic, multicultural society, yet simultaneously we hear that the schools are neglecting fundamental US values (Bennett 1992, Capper 1993, Chavkin 1993, Ravitch 1995). Elsewhere the paradoxical assertion is made that while teachers feel powerless to alter the ways schools operate, school administrators and school board members feel hamstrung by union contracts. Political pressures from the community hamper school administrators, yet many citizens feel that public schools are operated by school professionals for their own personal benefit (Kerchner and Mitchell 1988, Kerchner and Koppich 1993). Finally, persons of colour and the poor believe that public schools are neglecting their children's needs, killing their aspirations, while the affluent believe that schools have deteriorated beyond hope because they cater to problems of the least prepared (Berliner and Biddle 1995). How can we hope to reconcile these paradoxes?

A clue rests within competing purposes for education. Aristotle, among others, taught us that discussions about education are always contentious because an individual's view of the proper purposes and goals of education are highly dependent upon his/her conception of what constitutes the 'good life' (Everson 1988: Book vii). The resolution of this question concerning the constitution of the good life is the solution to identifying the purposes of education and depends on political philosophy. As I will explore below, Lowi (1995) provides us with some insight on various perspectives on this dilemma.

People hold different views of the relative success or failure of the public schools because they attribute bases for legitimacy of schools, if we use legitimacy to mean a fundamental view that an institution is working properly (Ward 1987). Whether an institution is working appropriately is both an empirical and a normative question.

One example of tensions surrounding legitimacy is the frequent call to return to the 'family values' of what have been termed the 'good old days', often situated in the 1950s. One critic of this view points out that the prevalent value structure of the 1950s openly and actively discriminated against African Americans and other minori-

0268–0939/97 $12 · 00 © 1997 Taylor & Francis Ltd.

ties, held women in social and economic subjugation and denied them reproductive freedom, under-served people with disabilities and hid them from view, allowed the terrorism of homosexuals and forced them to lead hidden and secret lives, and limited free speech through loyalty oaths for public employees (Glaser 1995). Whether the 1950s should be regarded as the high point of 'family values' depends upon one's view of the good life.

The issue of legitimacy and school performance

How schools deal with issues affecting the legitimacy of the public schools is illustrated through a parallel argument from public administration:

> The legitimacy of US public administration rests on the legitimacy of the political community itself and the administrators' ability to serve and represent that community. In the USA this sense of political community has been severely eroded by the extreme pluralism that characterises contemporary US politics. Therefore, public administrators can play a significant role in rebuilding their own legitimacy to the degree they can help restore a shared sense of political community at all levels of our political system. (Kass 1990: 12)

By analogy, a school administrator could restore legitimacy to a public school system through the development of political community that builds a working consensus on the purposes and goals of public education. Even so, questions remain about the extent of this political community. Can it be created in a school attendance area? A school district? A state district? The nation? These important questions may have no easy answers, but this chapter explores both the motivation and strategies for establishing political community in the interest of school legitimacy.

Waldo reminds us that all administration is based on political theory (Waldo 1984). Political theory drives our views toward what is proper in administration, but education is very much 'a contested public good' in the USA and 'historical perspective suggests that the current reform initiatives will continue to be ephemeral if they fail to engage the long-standing social accords that shape the life of schools' (James 1991: 170). Those 'longstanding social accords' are constituted from ideology and political theory. An examination of political theory and dominant political ideologies may resolve these paradoxes and provide some insight into policy making and administration in education.

Political ideology and theories of politics

Political scientist Theodore Lowi argues that political ideologies in the USA can be divided into liberal and conservative ideologies (Lowi 1995: 11–15). Lowi's use of 'liberal' and 'conservative' to describe basic political ideologies does not necessarily coincide with everyday use of the terms in political discourse.

Lowi attributes five defining characteristics to liberalism.

1. An emphasis on the individual, especially the individual in opposition to the collectivity, is the single most defining attribute of liberalism.
2. Liberalism focuses on individual wants and the satisfaction of those wants.
3. Liberalism is characterized by 'its steadfast opposition to the involvement of morality in public discourse' (Lowi 1995: 13).

4. In liberalism, the linkage between the individual and the collectivity is the social contract.
5. Liberalism is by definition anti-government and sees the major function of government as intervening against 'conduct deemed harmful or injurious in its consequences' (Lowi 1995: 15).

Liberalism has an affinity toward science and Lowi gives as example of heavy reliance on science liberal opposition to segregation as not based on moral grounds, but on the grounds of the consequences of segregation (Lowi 1995: 16). According to Lowi, if pluralism is the official political theory of liberalism, then Keynesian economics is the official economic theory of liberalism (Lowi 1995: 17).

Lowi further distinguishes between New Liberalism and Old Liberalism. New Liberalism has a lower threshold for government intervention. Lowi characterizes Old Liberalism as favoring a society free of risk and New Liberalism by a society free from risk. New Liberalism departed from Old Liberalism on the issue of at what point government intervention is justified. In New Liberalism, *laissez-faire* free markets and a libertarian philosophy are replaced by Keynesian economics and progressive state-ism. The New Liberalism in the period of the 1940s to the 1960s added to government programmes for social and economic justice regulatory power and redistribution programmes, thus lowering the risk assumed by the citizenry.

There are also five defining attributes of Conservatism, according to Lowi.

1. Conservatism is defined by a subordination of the individual to the collectivity.
2. Conservatives believe that individual pursuit of wants is wrong and religion exists to curb individual wants.
3. Conservatives also assert that moral truth can be known (it is often contained in religious texts) and society can impose morality on individuals, by law if necessary.
4. Society is not so much the result of a social contract, but it is the product of a natural order, according to Conservative ideology.
5. Government exists, according to Conservatives, to impose moral order for the attainment of a good society (Lowi 1995: 23–27).

Lowi also describes a difference between Old and New Conservatism. New Conservatism replaces the Old Conservative ideal of the good society with the ideal of a strong and virtuous society and emphasizes stateist conservatism over the traditional right and the old Christian right. Old Conservatism justifies government intervention in conduct that is *per se* good or evil, that is intervention for imposition of morality, while New Conservatism accepts an activist role for government to build a strong and virtuous society. Lowi also identifies a patrician strand in conservatism, which is more upper-class and based on private property and capitalism. He then names the populist strand for a lower-class conservatism normed on religious values and individualism.

Lowi posits that at least from the New Deal to the 1970s, both major political parties in the USA were liberal in ideology, only differing in degree on many issues. Whether that will continue to be true with the 'Republican Revolution of 1994' and the Contract With America remains to be seen.

Lowi argues that liberalism collapsed because of its overexpansion, leading to a regulatory and welfare state where any indication of future harm would provoke governmental intervention and the transformation of goals into rights. The conservative reaction against this led to the end of the liberal state (Lowi 1995: 44–79).

These political ideologies are also important in understanding differing views toward educational policy issues and the politics of education.

New Liberalism and education reform: context for the 1990s

The period of the 1960s, marked by President Lyndon B. Johnson's Great Society programme, was a time of intensive education reforms, of which the Elementary and Secondary Education Act of 1965 may be the most notable. Gibboney (1994) has characterized many of the reforms in the 1960s and 1970s as technological reforms, focusing on, among other programmes, compensatory education for the economically disadvantaged, foreign languages laboratories, computer-assisted instruction, new educational rights for the limited English proficient and the handicapped, individually prescribed instruction, mastery learning, and new testing programmes. Technological reforms clearly have been state interventionist, often with very large budgets attached, and designed to cushion children from risk. Technologial reforms are based on the liberal faith in science buttressed by notions of scientific management and ample research from behaviourism of 1950s and 1960s social science. Overall, there were few critics of technological reform among social scientists of the day, although sociologist C. Wright Mills was critical of the intellectual emptiness of what he terms the 'abstracted empiricism' of his day (Mills 1959) and some labelled these efforts as social engineering.

Such reforms were ideologically embedded in New Liberalism and ultimately engendered a reaction to what was perceived as excessive regulation and wasteful redistribution. The historical even that marked the end of this era of large-scale technological reform in the liberal tradition was the publication in 1983 of *A Nation at Risk* (National Commission on Excellence in Education 1983). *A Nation at Risk* challenged the underlying ideology of US educational reform charging that US public education had failed to live up to its promise and that this failure was reponsible for the declining position of the USA in global markets.

Ideology, political theory, and education reform

Many of the educational reforms proposed during the 1990s have been reactions against the regulatory and redistributive policies of the New Liberalism. However, a tension in this reaction is whether educational policy should revert to the Old Liberalism with its libertarian, free market bias, or to New Conservatism with its moral state-ism. Numerous examples of current initiatives illustrate this tension.

The reform called charter schools permit schools to operate at public expense but with minimum state regulation. Old Liberals find charter schools appealing due to maximization of local freedom in educational decisions and increased competition among schools. Charter schools appeal to some New Conservatives because they see relaxed state regulation as an opportunity to stress the values of Western civilization such as objective morality and building of community. Opposition to charter schools has come primarily from New Liberals, often led by teacher unions, who are unwilling to give up the regulations, rights or entitlements provided by state-dominated schools or to sacrifice their individual professional rights to the community.

This apparent commonality of interest around charter schools by Old Liberals and New Conservatives breaks down when the attention turns to an issue like school prayer. Old Liberals, as well as New Liberals, oppose school prayer as an improper imposition of a singular view of morality upon the rest of society. Conservatives embrace school prayer as a way of restoring morality to the 'godless' public schools.

The movement toward national and state academic standards and stricter accountability systems presents an interesting political dilemma. New Liberals generally support these concepts as a way of protecting the rights of all students through regulation and for improving the education of disadvantaged students. Old Liberals are suspicious of the movement as a threat to local control and local liberties. Conservatives are somewhat equivocal. The notion of clear and rigorous standards appeals to their sense of imposition of objective morality in order to achieve a strong and virtuous society, but there is a concern about who sets the standards. In many states Conservatives have opposed the standards movement because of fears of New Liberal values being imposed on schools.

Our social accords are not clear and there is much ambiguity surrounding educational policy issues like these. Political ideology and political theory shape individual and the societal views of educational policy issues. This becomes evident in policy discussion around educational reform.

Is a restoration of legitimacy possible?

New Liberalism and its focus on social equity issues dominated US educational policy making in the decades of the 1960s and 1970s. Both the Civil Rights Movement and the War on Poverty embraced the ideology of New Liberalism and most educational reforms of that period centred on improving social equity and equal educational opporunity. Both regulation and redistribution were commonplace in reform initiatives. In the 1980s, the conversations turned from equity to excellence. The excellence movement never achieved the clarity of the equity movement because some viewed excellence as a route to equal educational opportunity and others saw it as elitist.

In a provocative analysis of the similarities and differences between the 'new Public Administration' movement, focusing on social equity, and the movement toward 'reinventing government', with its focus on entrepreneurship, efficiency, and productivity, Frederickson (1996) asks whether we can solve the health care dilemma in the USA through better management and answers in the negative (p. 268). In a similar manner, we can ask whether better management will solve our educational problems and are likely to answer in the same negative fashion. Improvements in education will not come from better management which strives to increase excellence, efficiency, or both, but from greater legitimacy of the system. Kass (1990) argues that rebuilding legitimacy requires restoration of a shared sense of political community, and if he is correct in his argument, then how can that shared sense of community be established in a diverse, contentious political climate?

Gibboney (1994) has demonstrated that those school reforms which have been the most successful in the USA in the last three decades are those that have focused on democratic and intellectual factors rather than technological factors. This is consistent with Frederickson's (1996) thesis that social equity is achieved through greater democratic participation in decision making and an active and engaged citizenry. One way of fostering greater democratic participation in educational policy making is to provide greater community control of schools as opposed to the more traditional professional control of schools. Far too often, the community (and sometimes school board members) are shut out of decision making in schools by an 'iron triangle' of district central office staff, building administrators, and teacher unions. Although these groups appear to be at odds, often they work in concert to maintain professional control of schools for their own convenience and comfort. After all, voters often fail to participate in public decision making not because they do not want to vote their own interest, but because they are denied the opportunity to participate in a meaningful manner (Fox 1996).

Shenk (1996) asserts that public schools in the USA 'provide a common space where, in a country fissured along lines of race and class, children of all backgrounds meet, interact, and learn to understand each other' (p. 9). Thus the question becomes whether establishing a legitimate shared political community requires looking at public schools in terms of common space.

Common space, translated into political terms, becomes a public sphere, which Dryzek (1990) argues has two facets or attributes: public discourse and holistic experimentation. Public discourse involves 'free and open communication in political life, oriented toward reciprocal understanding, trust, and hence an undistorted consensus' (Dryzek 1990: 38). Public discourse does not work well in a representative democratic system, but is more fitting for participatory democracy. Holistic experimentation strives for 'an improvement in the aspects of the group's condition considered relevant, upon reflection, by its members (rather than before the fact by some external experimenter)' (Dryzek 1990: 39). Such an approach to educational decision making may be appropriate because Dryzek argues that 'spaces exist for discursive designs to the extent dominant political and economic institutions are crumbling under the weight of their contradictions' (p. 77). The contradictions of the differing ideologies of Liberalism and Conservatism, fostering distinctive views of education based on differing definitions of the 'good life', threaten the legitimacy of public schools. Dryzek's alternative view stresses a public policy making process that emphasizes public debate about policy issues in self-governing political communities (Dryzek 1989: 100).

A discursive or deliberative democracy is characterized by public policy making which emphasizes (1) citizens retaining power of judgement over public matters, (2) decisions made by deliberative means rather than through the more traditional mechanisms of representative government such as majority rule, and (3) limits to unchallenged authority and power of formal institutions and professional experts (Warren 1996). Discursive or deliberative democracy requires an open forum for public discussion of important issues, where the participants are communicatively competent and participation is non-hierarchical, and where unequal power situations are not allowed (Dryzek 1990). This form of public discussion and decision making must have procedural safeguards, common ground for discussion, a fair degree of shared values and understandings, some measure of social equity, and equal access to information (Majone 1988). Everyone listens and everyone can speak. This approach to making public decisions is atypical of the usual mode of decision making in schools, where professionals dominate, both in terms of active participation and access to expertise, where the system is hierarchical and dissent is repressed, and where unequal power situations are not only tolerated but promoted by school professionals.

One current reform which satisfies the main criteria of discursive democracy is site-based decision making. Site-based decision making often is described as a management reform, but I argue it has potential for restoring legitimacy to public schools by creating common space for political discourse regarding schooling in the community. It is facilitative of citizen involvement in policy making, of responsiveness to community needs and values, and of redefining schooling in communities through holistic experimentation. Site-based decision making appeals to the Old Liberal value of localized decision making, the Conservative emphasis on community and values, and the New Liberal concern for equal educational opportunity. I am not suggesting that site-based decision making is a panacea nor that it is easy to implement, instead I offer it as a means for development of a shared political community and social accord thus restoring the legitimacy of public schools. The promotion of public discourse around education in a local political community promotes both democracy and intellectual discourse, and if Gibboney is correct, intellectual and democratic reform is more likely to succeed than technological tinkering.

As individual citizens in a political community share visions of the good life and debate and discuss alternative approaches to schooling, it is possible that common understandings may be reached and common values may also be developed. The direct participation of citizens in local education decisions will give them a stake in the consequences of those decisions. The greatest impediment to site-based decision making may be the 'iron triangle' of district-level administrators, principals, and teachers who see it as a threat to professional control of schools. However, the future of public schools, if they are not to be destroyed by vouchers and other moves toward privatization of schooling, may be in the rejection of professional control and the acceptance of citizen control through participatory democracy and public discourse. Only then may the legitimacy of public schools be restored.

Conclusion

Although numerous reform efforts have focused on school improvement, few have addressed the political legitimacy of schools. Site-based decision making could produce the kind of discursive or deliberative democracy that is necessary to help restore the legitimacy of the public education system. Legitimacy results from opportunities to bring together people from diverse political ideologies to discuss issues of common concern, to develop shared meanings, and to arrive at important educational decisions through an open and unconstrained system with communicative rationality. A critical factor in this process will be whether school administrators and teachers will provide the leadership that will help support a restoration of a shared sense of political community or whether they will strive mightily to maintain the status quo for their own benefit. If the latter case is true, the current battle of political ideologies will continue to erode the legitimacy of public schools and irrevocably lead to the demise of a broad-based public school system.

References

BENNETT, W. L. (1992) *The Devaluing Of America: The Fight For Our Culture And Our Children* (New York: Summit Books).

BERLINER, D. C. and BIDDLE, B. J. (1995) *The Manufactured Crisis: Myths, Fraud, And The Attack On America's Public Schools* (Reading, MA: Addison-Wesley).

BRACEY, G. W. (1996) International comparisons and the condition of American education. *Educational Researcher*, **25**(1), 5–11.

CAPPER, C. A. (ed.) (1993) *Educational Administration in A Pluralistic Society* (Albany, NY: SUNY Press).

CHAVKIN, N. F. (ed.) (1993) *Families And Schools in A Pluralistic Society* (Albany: State University of New York Press).

DRYZEK, J. S. (1989) Policy science of democracy. *Polity*, 22(1), 97–118.

DRYZEK, J. S. (1990) *Discursive Democracy: Politics, Policy, and Political Science* (New York: Cambridge University Press).

EVERSON, S. (ed.) (1988) *Aristotle: The Politics* (New York: Cambridge University Press).

FOX, C. J. (1996) Reinventing government as postmodern symbolic politics. *Public Administration Review*, 56(3), 256–261.

FREDERICKSON, H. G. (1996) Comparing the reinventing government movement with the new public administration. *Public Administration Review*, 56(3), 263–270.

GIBBONEY, R. A. (1994) *The Stone Trumpet: A Story Of Practical School Reform 1960–1995* (Albany, New York: SUNY Press).

GLASER, I. (1995) Why go back to the immoral '50s?. *The Illinois Brief*, 52(4), 1, 7.

JAMES, T. (1991) State authority and the politics of educational change, in *Review Of Educational Research* (Washington, DC: American Educational Research Association), 17.

KASS, H. D. (1990) *Prologue: Emerging Issues And Themes In The Re-Examination Of American Public Administration, In Images And Identities In Pubic Administration* (Newbury Park, CA: Sage Publications).

KERCHNER, C. T. and KOPPICH, J. E. (1993) *A Union of Professionals: Labor Relations And Educational Reform* (New York: Teachers College Press).

KERCHNER, C. T. and MITCHELL, D. E. (1988) *The Changing Idea of A Teachers' Union* (London: Falmer).

LOWI, T. J. (1995) *The End Of The Republican Era* (Norman, OK: University of Oklahoma Press).

MILLS, C. W. (1959) *The Sociological Imagination* (New York: Oxford University Press).

MAJONE, G. (1988) Policy analysis and public deliberation, in R. B. Reich (ed.), *The Power Of Public Ideas* (Cambridge, MA: Harvard University Press).

NATIONAL COMMISSION ON EXCELLENCE IN EDUCATION (1983) *A Nation At Risk: The Imperative For Education Reform* (Washington, DC: US Department Of Education).

RAVITCH, D. (1995) *National Standards in American Education: A Citizen's Guide* (Washington: Brookins Institution).

SHENK, J. W. (1996) The public schools' last hurrah? *The Washington Monthly*, 28(3), 8–17.

WALDO, D. (1984) *The Administrative State: A Study Of The Political Theory Of American Public Administration*, 2nd edn (New York: Holmes & Meier Publishers).

WARD, J. G. (1987) An inquiry into the normative foundations of American public school finance. *Journal of Educational Finance*, 12, 463–477.

WARREN, M. E. (1996) Deliberative democracy and authority. *American Political Science Review*, 90(1), 46–60.

Part 2

4.   *The microecology of school–community links*

Hanne B. Mawhinney, University of Ottawa, and
Charles Kerchner, Claremont Graduate School

This chapter demands that we rethink our conceptions of partnerships in fostering eduational change. Our intention is to further the research agenda on the mechanisms proposed by proponents of the communitarian model of schooling for building community capacity. We set out an orienting framework on the implications of ecology-of-games. Our orientation to school–community links takes direction from Kerchner's (1995) proposal for understanding the capacity of schools to generate economic and social renewal in their communities. We show that the challenges raised by a conception of schools as basic industry pose analytical and methodological problems in bounding cases of school–community links which turn us to seek guidance from the insights offered by Long (1958) into the ecology-of-games, and to Hawley's more recent explication of the human ecology paradigm (1968, 1986). Based on an analytical framework of ecological organization developed from this paradigm, we return to the challenge offered by Kerchner (1995). Finally, we call for an examination of different value frameworks aligned with metaphors of neighborliness, intergenerational responsibility, ecological interdependence, and privatization.

Reconstituting a communitarian model of public schooling

For the past decade, public schooling in North America has undergone revision, reform, and restructuring. Despite the range of change efforts, pressures for reform continue. Murphy and Hallinger (1992) list among the 'pressures for reform' increasing importance of education, competitive forces in the global market, demands of a changing population, the changing political landscape, the debureaucratization of society, and the decentralization of problems. The scope of these pressures is such that they have caused a fundamental rethinking of the institution of public schooling, and particularly the relations of schools to their communities (Crowson 1992, Cibulka and Kritek 1996, Driscoll 1996, Goldring 1996).

An impetus to school reform is the new 'communitarian model of schooling' which views schools as 'small societies', as organizations that emphasize informal and enduring social relationships and are driven by a common ethos' (Lee *et al.* 1993: 173). Communitarian critics of schools emphasize the dysfunction of a bureaucratic organization of schooling. They call instead for a 'strengthening of social ties between students and adults around the educational activities of the school' (p. 174). In practise this model has embraced several different dimensions of school–community relations. One dimension of this model supports parental participation in the schooling of their children through 'enforcing normative standards concerning education

0268–0939/97 $12 · 00 © 1997 Taylor & Francis Ltd.

and . . . through monitoring and planning the educational experience of their children' (p. 190).

Another impetus for strenthening of school–family ties is found in Coleman and Hoffer's (1987) conception of functional communities which support cross-generational ties between parents and children. They argue that these communities provide unique social capital which facilitates the work of the school. Other research confirms the positive consequences for children and teachers of parental volunteer efforts (Lee *et al.* 1993). Chubb (1988) also concludes that 'all things being equal, schools in which parents are highly involved, cooperative, and well-informed are more likely to develop effective organizations than schools in which parents do not possess these qualities' (p. 40).

The current emphasis on strengthening family–school relations is arguably a reinvention, given the long history of 'community schools' in the USA (Katz 1973, Epstein 1995) and Canada (Mawhinney 1993 and 1996). In its current form this perspective 'addresses the deinstitutionalization of urban neighborhoods and their declining capacity to support healthy family life' (Lee *et al.* 1993: 192). Schools are seen as sites for reconstituting communities. For example, Comer's (1980) New Haven schools create functional communities building alliances between families, school staff, children and others important to the education of the child.

Other models focus on structural aspects of community control of schools through site-based governance plans. Supporters of these new governance plans believe that schools can best be made more responsive to the needs of children if there is greater collaborative decision making between parents and school personnel. Some proposals take the form of school-based governance by parents. Proponents of school-based management support a shift of governance to local districts and school sites and the participation of parents, community members, and older students in decision-making structures.

Similar trends to decentralize decision making and accountability are found in health and social service systems where efforts are underway to provide local communities with 'the flexibility, authority, and resources they need to develop strategies for service delivery that address the problems and meet the needs of their children and families' (Mutchler *et al.* 1993: 9). These thrusts do not reflect a return to nineteenth-century models of service delivery which were supported solely by community groups. The policy frameworks support community ownership and involvement in planning, organizing and implementing new service systems. They also rely on the expertise and experience of education, health, social services, and other professionals. Many state and provincial governments recognize that community involvement in developing and governing new social service systems is essential (Mutchler *et al.* 1993).

A growing array of local governance structures, which include new mechanisms for building community capacity, have been developed in response to perceived discontinuities in the system of social institutions supporting children and families. Many states and provinces have put in place policy frameworks to support community governance structures. As part of the new agenda for reinventing government these initiatives adopt strategies directed at developing the capacity of communities, rather than single institutions, to meet the needs of families and children (Mawhinney 1993). Proponents of community capacity building reject traditional conceptions of clients who are served, or who wait for others to address their needs. Instead, they propose an agenda of empowerment, gives ownership of problems to

citizens, who 'understand their own problems in their own terms...[and who] perceive their relationshp to one another and believe in their capacity to act' (Osborne
and Gaebler 1992: 52).

Changing the conversation about education and community

The heralded outcomes of rediscovering the strengths of community appear impress-
ive: commitment, understanding of local problems, a problem-solving rather than
service-provision orientation, caring, flexibility and creativity, efficiency, shared
values, and a focus on human capacity over deficiency. In recent years politics of education scholars have developed new conceptual approaches to building community
capacity. Kerchner (1995) suggests that educational analysts have been hampered in
this effort by the widespread crisis rhetoric which has intensified their policy attention
around rescuing schools from collapse and failure (p. 2). He observes, however, that
the focus on righting an apparently failed social service system cannot turn the discourse from despair to hope. Kerchner argues that educational analysts have been led
astray by attacks focused on the function of public education in contemporary cities,
and lays out a logic of changing premises about school reform from failure to urban
development. Conception of schools as a basic industry in modern cities is a central
element of this new logic. Education, Kerchner argues, 'needs to be seen, and needs
to function, as a basic industry: that which multiplies investments, attracts people
and capital, a builder of modern cities rather than an expensive social programme'
(p. 3). Schools build cities, and, thus, communities in two ways:

> They develop the economy both indirectly, by adding to a location's stock of human capital, and directly,
> through programmes that enhance neighborhoods. Schools become part of a micro-economic policy. Good
> schools serve as agents for community development, the creation of cohesion, and positive civic relations
> among neighbors. (p. 3)

Kerchner's proposals respond to the problems of schooling in US cities which are
now commonly seen as 'a refuge for the poor and the host to an apocalyptical vision
of class warfare' (p. 6). His analysis is broader, focusing on the influences of macro
forces of world globalization on the emergence of independent economic and social
functions of cities. New theorizing on the role of 'global cities' has underlined their
capacity to function as highly concentrated command points in the world economy.
Education is among the investments, both public and private, that produce an innovative synergy in uniquely 'global cities' like Tokyo, and New York. Kerchner goes
so far as to argue that 'cities are utterly dependent on an education system in order to
rebuild their neighborhoods' (p. 9).

Although the evident connection between cities and schools has been acknowledged by educational analysts, Kerchner proposes that viewing schools as basic industries enables explorations of more instrumental and purposive connections between
schools and communities. He describes connections that link schools with economic
development through efforts to customize training, to engage in direct technical assistance, and to act as labor market intermediaries. Kerchner identifies a second type of
connection, one in which schools become creators of communities through specific
strategies that demonstrate consensus building to overcome conflict, rebuild community pride, provide a locus for family services, and create a place for training in democracy.

Revisiting the problem of embeddedness of action and institutions in social relations

Kerchner posits that these strategies can best be fostered by developing infrastructures for small schools which rationalize governance processes freeing local sites to make the decisions they must. In doing so he raises some of the sticky methodological problems faced by researchers seeking to understand how context matters in school organization and local decision making.

Although the problem of the embeddedness of behaviour and institutions in the structures of social relations is one of the classic questions in social theory, it continues to bedevil the efforts of educational analysts who, like Kerchner, offer analytical lenses for capturing the dynamics of school–community links. In examining embedded social action, many within the broader disciplines of sociology and political science have confronted conceptual problems posed by assumptions of rationality underlying early thinking about individual and organizational behavioural models of decision making and economic action. In recent years the revised assumption of constrained rationality has become widely accepted by social theorists. For example, in tackling the analytical problem of embeddedness of economic action in the structure of social relations, Granovetter (1985) concludes that 'while the assumption of rational action must always be problematic, it is a good working hypothesis that should not easily be abandoned. What looks to the analyst like nonrational behaviour may be quite sensible when situational constraints, especially those of embeddedness, are fully appreciated' (p. 506).

Granovetter's analysis of the power of contextual forces is widely recognized by educational researchers. The problem is how to conceptually bound a context under study when it is fluid. Well's (1996) and her colleagues underline the challenges confronted by educational researchers studying schools where 'change continuously occurs–personnel come and go, policies are enacted, respondents' views of reform shift, and political action takes on new and different forms' (p. 23). Their analysis of the problems of examining the politics of local context points to the need for analytical frames which capture the ecological rationality of social interaction structures, such as those offered by political scientists like Long (1958), and sociologists like Hawley (1986). Their analysis offers us a lens with which to examine problems of reinventing partnerships for educational change.

Towards an ecological orientation to examining community links

Conceptions of ecology guide sociological theorizing on ecological organization from early work on human ecology. US sociologists like Park (1929) applied concepts from bio-ecology such as community, dominance and succession to the study of human ecology, and recently Hawley (1950, 1968, 1986), has been one of the leading theorists of human ecology. These studies focused on the 'way human populations organize in order to maintain themselves in given environments' (Hawley 1986: 3). Early versions of human ecology became associated with 'the study of the form and development of the human community' (Hawley 1950: 68). Over the years the concept of human community came to be seen as 'territorially localised system of relationships among functionally differentiated parts' (Hawley 1968: 329).

Recently Hawley (1986) has argued that the most important contribution of bio-ecology to human ecology has been 'the perspective of collective life as an adaptive process consisting of an interaction of environment, population, and organization' (p. 4). The concept of ecosystem, which denotes 'an association of species and its environment between which energy and information are regularly cycled', emerges from this perspective (p. 4).

A fundamental assumption of human ecology is that adaptation proceeds through interdependencies among members of a population. Hawley (1986) suggests that a human population is an aggregate of individuals who possess five basic characteristics: 'a necessity for environmental access, inescapable interdependence, inherent expansiveness, temporal constraint, and variability of behaviour with indeterminate limits' (p. 125). These fundamental attributes define ecological organization, and its central concept of 'niche', which connotes 'resource space and is regarded as a variable property of environment' (p. xiv). Organizations are considered by some ecologists to be limited in their ability to adapt their internal forms to different niches. This school of organizational ecology points to strong inert organizational forces which limit the amount and degree of change possible. Structural inertia results from factors such as sunk costs, historical precedent, and political resistance to change (Hannan and Freeman 1977).

The utility and analytical power of the organizational ecology perspective derives from its capacity to account for both institutional and ecological variables. Hawley (1986) argues, for example, that through the key element 'environment', 'organizational ecology takes into account not only institutions, but also a body of rules, an ideology, and the attributes of client populations' (p. xv). These characteristics are shared by the human ecology perspective. However, human ecology also incorporates a collective action perspective which argues that organizations 'symbiotically collude to ensure the continued existence of the interorganizational network as a whole' (Astley and Van de Ven 1983: 259). Human ecology, through its emphasis on cooperation, recognizes the 'importance of social and political rather than economic forces' (p. 259). Cooperation is found in symbiotic relationships in the interactions between the organization performing the key function in a niche, and the other organizations for which it mediates the environment.

The recognition that power plays a role in this relationship underlines the importance of political forces. Inherent in this role is the power of regulation over other networks. At the same time, power relations become more complete as interorganizational networks fill their resource space and approach closure (Hawley 1968). As this occurs, political negotiation plays an increasingly important role in regulating the flow of economic resources throughout the network (Astley and Van de Ven 1983: 260). In this way, human ecology assumes a collective action orientation, characterized by conflict, negotiation, and compromise. Human behaviour such as occurs in forming school–community links is collectively constructed and politically negotiated. Change occurs through both conflict and compromise, through negotiation and partisan mutual adjustment. In this view an ecosystem comprizes communities or networks of 'semi autonomous partisan groups that interact to modify or construct their collective environment, rules, and options' (p. 247). Collective action is viewed as not only controlling, but also liberating and expanding individual action.

The human ecology perspective gives weight to the utility of viewing partnerships for educational change as embedded in an ecology-of-games involving interdependencies between multiple actors, first set out by Norton Long (1958). Long's conception of the community as an ecology-of-games, based on a year's field study in Boston, is considered among the outstanding contributions to sociological literature between 1925 and 1950. The themes Long develops are based on his fundamental concern with how a democratic society achieves its goals. Long argues that a local community, whether viewed as a polity, as an economy, or as a society, reflects 'an order in which expectations are met and functions performed' (p. 251). This order does not arise from the impositions of some centralized point of control, but rather it is the product of a history of interactions among many institutions, including local government departments, agencies of the states and the federal government, banks, newspapers, trade unions, churches and others. Long argues that in interacting with each other, these institutions form a system where inclusive and 'overall organization for many general purposes is weak or non-existence' (p. 252). What occurs, he argues, is more the result of 'accidental trends becoming cumulative over time and producing results intended by nobody' (p. 252).

Methodological and analytical issues in contextualizing cases

Long's conception of the community as an ecology-of-games is a useful counterpoint for an analysis of Kerchner's conception of schools as basic industries. Along with the human ecology perspective it can guide an examination of the forces giving impetus to the different value frameworks defining the links betwen schools and their communities. The ecological perspective illuminates researchers' understanding of how context matters. It enables us to tackle the difficulty of 'bounding a case within its context' (Wells *et al*. 1995).

Long's ecological perspective offers a metaphor for directing our analytical gaze beyond traditional boundaries found in research on the local politics of education. Much of this research was conducted in the 1960s and 1970s, and while offering some valuable lessons on the influential role of local context in educational change, it does not fully capture the interconnectedness of local, district and community power struggles with what happens in schools, and with the agency of educators in classrooms. In taking an ecological thrust we move away from the commonly adopted 'organizational model' of school systems which has compelled educational policy analysts to view the connections between schools, their districts and the state policy structures as loosely coupled.

We believe that organizational bias in politics of education scholarship has underestimated the importance of local political context. Moreover, it has not provided the analytical guidance to develop a more normative or interpretive understanding of district-level politics and policy making. Others have noted the need to study the interplay of competing ideologies in defining the 'what?' of the politics of education at the local level (Stout *et al*. 1995: 5). However, the turn from local politics to the study of state and federal policy making by educational analysts during the past two decades has been weakly explored. Although politics of education scholarship has told us something about the functioning of school boards, the literature does not provide guidance for those seeking to 'bound' case studies which attempt to capture the embeddedness of schools in the context of prevailing community politics and norms as Wells *et al*. (1995) point out.

Conclusion

The ecological perspective suggested by both Long (1958) and Hawley (1986) offers an approach which can capture some of this embeddedness. We believe that this approach holds potential for researchers wishing to analyse the of micro-ecological accommodation to which Kerchner (1995) draws our attention. There is value in an approach which links the emerging themes of reconstruction and renewal that can be found if we analyse the embeddedness of the schools in the microecology of their communities. Within these themes can be found value frameworks similar to the two orientations Kerchner suggests schools can take in generating community growth and development. The first is an orientation taken by the school which promotes economic development through efforts to customize training, to engage in direct technical assistance, and to act as labor market intermediaries. Kerchner identifies a second orientation, one in which schools become creators of communities through specific strategies that demonstrate consensus building to overcome conflict, that rebuild community pride, provide a locus for family services, and that create a place for training in democracy.

In this chapter we have argued for an approach which focuses on the value frameworks supporting community development and economic renewal evident in these two orientations. It is an orientation to understanding the stance toward communities taken by schools which captures the embeddedness of their efforts in the microecology of social relations. Our analysis supports the value of viewing schools as basic industries set out by Kerchner. We claim that this approach focuses attention on themes of neighborliness, integenerational responsibilty, privtization and ecologial interdependence evident in accounts educators give of the efforts of schools to form stronger links with their communities. Together these themes call for an ecological orientation to understanding the organizational changes that occur as a result of these links. Viewed from the lens of human ecology, managing the microecology of school–community links requires an awareness that partnerships are constructed of a loose web of interrelationships that are embedded in a unique context, defined in part by an attentive public. Ecologists describe the potential variability of responses to collaborative efforts and the time-bound nature of the involvement of individual players. These and other propositions about the nature of ecological relationshps offer an analytical frame with which to examine the potential of systemic reforms to create coherence. We offer them as a contribution to the dialogue on the potential of educational reforms to generate the coherence required for change to occur.

References

ASTLEY, G. W. and VAN DE VEN, A. H. (1983) Central perspectives and debates in the organizational theory. *Administrative Science Quarterly*, **28**, 245–273.

CHUBB, J. E. (1988) Why the current wave of school reform will fail. *The Public Interest*, **90**, 28–49.

CIBULKA, J. G. and KRITEK, W. J. (1996) *Coordination Among Schools, Families, and Communities: Prospects For Educational Reform* (Albany, NY: SUNY Press).

COLEMAN, J. and HOFFER, T. (1987) *Public And Private High Schools: The Impact Of Communities* (New York: Basic Books).

COMER, J. (1980) *School Power: Implication Of An Intervention Project* (New York: Free Press).

CROWSON, R. L. (1992) *School–Community Relations, Under Reform* (Berkeley: McCutchan).

DRISCOLL, M. E. (1996) The new institutionalism and the new communitarianism: implications for school reform, in W. L. Boyd, R. L. Crowson and H. B. Mawhinney (eds), *The Politics Of Education And The New Institutionalism: Reinventing The American School* (Washington: Falmer).

EPSTEIN, J. (1995) School/family/community partnerships: caring for the children we share. *Phi Delta Kappan,* **76**, 701–712.

GRANOVETTER, M. (1985) Economic action and social structure: The problem of embeddedness. *American Journal of Sociology,* **91**, 481–510.

GOLDRING, E. B. (1996) Institutionalism and adaptation, in W. L. Boyd, R. L. Crowson and H. B. Mawhinney (eds), *The Politics Of Education And The New Institutionalism: Reinventing The American School* (Washington: Falmer).

HANNAN, M. and FREEMAN, J. (1977) The population ecology of organizations. *American Journal of Sociology,* **82**, 929–964.

HAWLEY, A. H. (1950 *Human Ecology: A Theory of Community Structure* (New York: Ronald).

HAWLEY, A. H. (1968) Human ecology, in D. Sills (ed.), *International Encyclopedia of Social Sciences,* Vol. 4 (New York: Free Press), 328–337.

HAWLEY, A. H. (1986) *Human Ecology: A Theoretical Essay* (Chicago: University of Chicago Press).

KATZ, M. B. (1973) *Education In American History: Readings On The Social Issues* (New York: Praeger).

KERCHNER, C. T. (1995) *Rethinking City Schools: An Introduction. The California Education Policy Seminar* (Working Paper 1).

LEE, V. E., BRYK, A. S. and SMITH, J. B. (1993) The organization of effective secondary schools, in L. Darling-Hammond (ed.), *Review of Educational Research,* 171–267.

LONG, N. E. (1958) The local community as an ecology-of-games. *American Journal of Sociology,* **50**, 251–261.

MAWHINNEY, H. B. (1993) Discovering shared values: ecological models to support interagency collaboration, in L. Adler and S. Gardner (eds), *The Politics of Linking Schools and Social Services* (Washington: Falmer Press), 33–47.

MAWHINNEY, H. B. (1996) Institutional effects of strategic efforts at community enrichment, in J. G. Cibulka and W. J. Kritek (eds), *Coordination Among Schools, Families, And Communities: Prospects For Educational Reform* (Albany: SUNY Press), 223–243.

MURPHY, J. (1991) *Restructuring Schools: Capturing And Assessing The Phenomenon* (New York: Teachers College Press).

MURPHY, J. and HALLINGER, P. (1992) The principalship in an era of transformation. *Journal of Educational Administration,* **30**, 77–88.

MUTCHLER, S. E., MAYS, J. L. and POLLARD, J. S. (1993) *Finding Common Ground: Creating Governance Structures* (Austin TX: Southwest Educational Development Laboratory).

OSBORNE, D. and GAEBLER, T. (1992) *Reinventing Government* (Reading, MA: Addison Wesley).

PARK, R. (1929) Sociology, community and society, in W. Gee (ed.), *Research In The Social Sciences* (New York: Macmillan).

STOUT, R. T., TALLERICO, M. and SCRIBNER, K. P. (1995) Values: the 'what?' of the politics of education, in J. D. Scribner and D. H. Layton (eds), *The Study Of Educational Politics* (London: Falmer), 5–20.

WELLS, A. S., Hirshberg, D., Lipton, M. and Oakes, J. (1995) Bounding the case within its context: a constructivist approach to studying detracking reform, *Educational Researcher,* **24**(5), 18–24.

5. *Schools and their community: tensions and tradeoffs*

Stephen Crump
University of Sydney, Australia

In this Chapter I will explore whether parents feel they influence schools' community participation. This topic has been 'hot' in most developed nations throughout the 1990s (overlapping political as well as geographical borders) and also has been a key ingredient in reforms in the new countries of Central Europe. As such, education policy–intended or in practise–provides a context where the politics of education emerges with tensions that arise, tradeoffs made, and is at its most transparent. This chapter reports research from Sydney, Australia, with nearly 100 teachers and 700 families in a neighborhood community (Crump and Eltris 1995a, 1995b). This research is part of a broader work with the Institue for Responsive Education and the League of Schools Reaching Out based at Boston University. The chapter thus reports on the intent and practise of recent policy initiatives designed to refom the connections between school and home into a stronger sense of partnership (See Frutcher *et al.* 1993).

The immediacy of these issues in current public policy suggests a practical political problem for policy decision makers, school personnel, families and communities as they struggle to define what is intended, who is in control and who benefits. However, many such strategies are quick-fix solutions (i.e. a 'policy burlesque'; Crump 1993). Rarely are teachers, families and employers allowed to share perspectives or become involved in a period of research and development on programmes in a supportive educational environment. Rarely are staff or families prepared for more open, two-way school–home connections. This failure to locate the levels of preparedness of those affected by the programme alerts us to an analysis of the initial 'problem' that at worst has ignored the micro-political implications; or at least revealed naive minimal expectation about the consequential shifts in authority and control within the school; as well as between the school and its community during the following implementation (Berg 1993). Indeed, the rationale for many of these programmes assumes at least a neutral political context. Programmes rarely build their strategies on the notion that there may be a negative reaction that is highly political and complex and that is multiplied through the various interest groups within and without schools and their communities (local, regional and state). Yet complex reaction is politically inevitable and quite common in public policy in and beyond education (Crump 1992a, 1992b). Therefore, we ask, where tensions exist, are there sufficient mechanisms of schooling to accommodate political pressures, i.e. tradeoffs?

Schools, communities and policy devolution in Australia

Parental and other community input to schools in Australia has been very limited this century though some states have had strong input from communities for the last decade or more. It should be noted that this is not necessarily a historical situation and public education began in Australia through strong community agitation, input and support (Cleverley 1971: 139). Further, the bureaucratization of schooling created awkward distinctions between the terms 'involvement' and 'participation' when describing the roles the community might play. Cuttance (1993) provides an illustration of this distinction:

> The term involvement is used to mean the practical support by community members of school activities through support within the classroom, support in the preparation of teaching aids, fund raising, assistance with sporting activities and excursions, or assistance with the development of the physical environment of the school. The term participation is used to mean taking active part in the decision-making processes of the school. (p. 11)

According to Johnson (1993: 30), effective implementation of policy documents is impeded by 'muddleheadedness' in the education bureaucracy. Another example provided by Johnson (1993: 28), while simultaneously deploring inaccuracy of terminology, restricts participants to PTA-type representatives which indicates an inadequate grasp of the different processes and principles required to support involvement and/or participation.

From our perspective (Crump and Eltis 1995a, 1995b), it is mistaken to view participation-involvement as an either/or proposition. Our project viewed involvement-participation as a continuum with alternative strategies appropriate for alternative issues, problems or contexts satisfying micro- and meso-political imperatives. Such a construction makes possible a return to the unfulfilled democratic purposes of public education.

Perspectives and players

As recent research has shown (Ball 1994), it is one thing to assert policy, it is another to ask a large organization to respond in a meaningful and faithful manner to a set of priorities devised at the top, then filtered down through a diverse and fragmented system. What is worse, better school–home links priorities are 'off the agenda' in current New South Wales (NSW) following the emergence of a strong centralist state government. As schools are drawn in new policy directions by state administration, it will take high-order political skills for teachers and community allies who wish to maintain school–home connections as a central concern. The transience of policy initiatives, regardless of the degree of support and financial resources, and regardless of their levels of 'success', is one of the great political failures of contemporary education. Political expediency at the macro level sows mistrust and apathy in educational workers as well as confusion and complacency in electors and school communities.

Teacher unions' history in the school–community milieu is ambiguous and unimpressive. While the rhetoric about family/community input varies between enthusiasm and hostility from state to state in Australia, teacher unions actively block parent representation in areas the unions claim for teachers' professional privilege (see Iannaccone and Lutz [1995] for US comparison). In an unsigned article in *The Australian Educator* (1995: 9–12), the Australian Education Union expresses fears about unrepresentative groups who try to cross this line. The AEU position is for families/community to act in an advisory capacity only. But this is a weak claim on which unions and government attempt to assert their privilege over educational decision making (Glenn 1992). Hierarchical structures, line management and a focus on executive decision making within union bureaucracies, alongside endemic political in-fighting, render unions antagonistic to other educational interests. For unions, the struggle over education is ideological and a struggle against the state. In this context, any notion of partnership is anathema.

Yet, as teachers know from direct experience, there is little more important for education than home–community connections, regardless of social class, colour or religion. The exclusion of broader community perspectives about education is politically inappropriate in a democracy. Schools must be accountable for what they do and for children whose attendance is compelled by the state and who are taught and assessed on knowledge validated almost solely by the teaching profession. The next section will explore one study on neighborhood tensions and tradeoffs over school–home links.

Researching school–home connections

In 1992 I undertook a pilot study at my neighborhood school to ascertain the worth of a larger project on the nature and effectiveness of home–school connections in the district. The full project began early in 1994 (with Ken Eltis) with approval from regional administrators, school principals and the University of Sydney ethics committee followed by community input into the development of research instruments. A tangential study was conducted at the same time by Mawson (1994). The direction of the research was influenced by visits in 1992 and 1994 to the Institute for Responsive Education at Boston University, base for an international network committed to promoting the social and academic success of students through family–community–school collaboration. The forum for this network is The Centre on Families, Communities, Schools and Children's learning headed by Joyce Epstein and Don Davies. Our adaptation of the Epstein–Clark–Salinas Survey (John Hopkins University), served as the basis for the quantitative data collection. The research aims included:

- to determine and compare parent/teacher expectations in NSW government primary schools regarding the impact of mandated policy on school–home partnerships;
- to determine parents', teachers' and school leaders' judgments about the steering of school–home partnership strategies;
- to explore whether the state has replaced detailed rules with looser framework rules regarding education policy and to assess the impact of such changes on community participation.

The project was researched through a multi-method approach which accepts quantitative and qualitative methods as complementary. This approach sought both depth and breadth of data intending to construct, through triangulation of research strategies and techniqes, as full a picture as possible of the research aims. The theoretical orientation drew on the philosophical perspective of pragmatism, begun by Peirce, James and Mead, extended by Dewey and currently undergoing a third-generation revival in the USA (Rorty 1983, 1991, Cherryholmes 1994, Garrison 1994) and Australia

(Walker 1988, Evers 1993, Crump 1995). It was argued that the identification of shared meanings and common goals in school–home partnerships was most likely to arise through pragmatist principles tested through application to a real problem.

Profile of Baysview neighborhood

The Wangal Aboriginal people settled in the district at least 40,000 years ago calling it 'Wanne'. The area extended about 10 miles along the shores of the inner Sydney harbor from where European occupation began in 1788 (and now stand the Sydney Harbour Bridge and Opera House). Middens, piles of sea shells left where the Wangal had feasted, are a common reminder of this once vibrant culture. Following European invasion, the Wangal enjoyed friendly contact but as contact increased they attacked white settlers, burnt huts, and drove off stock. However, the Wangal community was soon decimated by disease and disposession. Baysview neighborhood in the 1990s is a collection of inner urban suburbs and schools serve a diverse socioeconomic, cultural and linguistic community living in homes that are apartments, houses on the waterfront, public commission dwellings or 'typical' Sydney family homes. School students are generally Anglo-Saxon Celtic or European, with high proportions of recent Asian and Arab immigrants. All schools are schools of choice with some children traveling from other neighborhoods to attend, for example, an elementary school with a predominant Sri Lankan or Chinese enrollment.

Survey data

Responses to the first research instrument–a four page survey–were evenly split between families with female and male pupils; 80% were filled in by the mother, 16% by the father and the rest by other relatives/guardians. In summary, 65% of parents/families marked 'YES' (Strongly Agree) teachers cared at their child's school and 33% marked 'yes' (Agree). Most indicated schools have an active Parents and Citizens Association (57%=YES; 37%=yes) though only 25% reported attending meetings. Most parents stated that they helped their child with writing, reading and mathematics though 82% (46%=YES; 36%=yes) responded they could help more if shown how. While 98% stated they talk to their child about school, 27% reported they had not visited their child's class and 26% had not talked to their child's teacher more than half-way through the school year. Significantly, 29% reported having different goals than the school for their children (Crump and Eltis 1995a).

This stage of the research suggested common ground between parents and teacher perspectives over central aspects of each school's daily activities, yet also evidenced tensions and tradeoffs. While families are active in their support of their own child and of the school, they appeared to be looking for more precise information about what occurs in classrooms so that they can help appropriately, and for more detailed explanations about assessment information. These data raised a number of factors sought through interview and document analysis including these issues:

- Which interest group(s) has/have authority over the forms of school activity?
- Which sources of authority are decisive?
- Whose (home or school) values dominate?

Interview and documentary data

The study gained a cross-section of views on home–school connections through a multiple set of data sources. School policy documents such as the Annual Report, the school plan for the years ahead, the weekly Newsletter, and the Homework Policy were reviewed. These documents portray a high degree of concern by school management for better home–school links. There are a number of factors influencing this built around a long-held belief in this aspect of schooling at the elementary level. This belief has been invigorated by the impact of market forces which mean that, amongst other consequences, if the school does not attract enrollments, it will lose staff or close down. School plans and annual reports from Bayview schools provide extensive detail on current practise including:

- parents as reading tutors at school and a more active home reading programme;
- formation of a School Council (though not with unanimous agreement);
- improved fund-raising;
- parent/coffee rooms initiated in three schools;
- communication through staff/parent committee work (with parents elected);
- increased in community languages included in the curriculum.

Interviews were conducted with parents and teachers. These interviews confirmed impressions gained from the documentary and survey data. While home–school connections have a high priority, there are areas where the concerns of the home and the school generated unresolved tensions. Further, other policy concerns have to be traded off in giving this the schools' attention. Teacher interviews and survey comments confirmed the item data which indicated a fairly evenly spread continuum from enthusiasm to disinterest amongst teachers about community participation as attested by these teacher comments:

> I generally appreciate seeing parents about the school to pick up children, doing canteen duty, on special days and talking informally of progress, work set and expectations…Some parents don't avail themselves of this opportunity to work together with the school, while others are available much more often and very interested. Usually, parents have some problems at school.

> Parents need to take responsibility for their child's upbringing and need to make them responsible for their own care–shoes, clothes–and become partners in training children to be responsible caring members of a group. Many children are coming to school with no self-help skills, poor social skills, little/no English and poor self-discipline. Parents need to be aware of the implications the lack of these skills may have on the educational development of their child.

Parent interviews confirmed findings from the survey that indicated the importance of school. We conducted interviews with over 40 families and believe that we achieved a representative cross-section. Parental concerns about school practises indicate the tension of strong support for their child's school against critical reflection about how various aspects could be improved. Families were prepared to enter in some tradeoffs. Underlying parents' comments is a view that they are just as accountable for their child's education but give teachers the right to educate and care for them in school time. This a serious, but largely ignored, political dimension for neighborhoods. Our respondents felt it is important that the neighborhood should have a sense of belonging to the school. Here are some of the parents comments.

> After 11 years at this school there is not much that we haven't been involved in.

> [This school] could explain in detail what is required by the students for homework and not expect parents to guess. Also, there is a need for a more updated way of parent and teacher discussing the needs of students.

On final consideration is the coherence, or common ground within a school over these issues: between executive teachers, between executive and classroom teachers, between teacher groups and families, between active and silent families (see Toomey 1996). At one of the Baysview schools we tracked the distinctions made between some of these sub-groups as follows:

> *Principal*: From my point of view, it is very exasperating if a message at home is contrary to what the teacher is trying to give at school and that I guess brings a community and a school into conflict. The parent community is out of step with the what the school is expecting. That is where the principal and the executive [teacher] come in, ensuring that they get into alignment. . .As principal my agenda for involving parents is to communicate a lot with parents about what is happening in the school. . .and they will get time off work and set that time aside for their children.

> *Assistant Principal*: I think that some teachers have very different view of parent participation [from parent perspectives] and what the school needs to do is to match what the parents' expectations are to what the teachers' are. . . It is a sharing. You realize that parents are the child's first teachers, they know the child better than anyone else. A lot of teachers discount that, they think they have all the answers. . . I think schools should be aware that parents are coming voluntarily and be flexible. They have other activities too, so if a parent can't come, don't make that parent feel guilty that they are apologizing.

> *Active Parent* (married, at home): [I undertook to be be interviewed] so I could express things that I probably haven't had the opportunity to express before and I think it is important for the powers that be at the school to get the views of parents. I don't think that has been attempted to any degree in the past. I find it difficult to know what the school is aiming for my child. . . Obviously the school is a caring school but I think parents need to know exactly how their child is progressing. I think it is a bit hard to kind of get a handle on exactly what the school thinks about your child.

> *Silent Parents* (working): [I agreed to be interviewed because] I want to know what is happening, mainly with the formation of the school council I have heard a lot of talk about, but I haven't actually seen that much [information], it hasn't made that much impact on me as a parent. . . Some teachers encourage it [participation/involvement] more than others and that could be how they feel your personality will fit in to theirs. Two or three have been fantastic. . .that's two or three [out of 14, their emphasis].

These quotes indicate how, despite overlapping perspectives about the importance of bringing home and school 'into alignment', there are significant differences between how that is to be done. The principal quite clearly expects parents to adhere to school's perspectives and this is how s(he) defines 'support'. Parents are expected to take time off work as the principal perceives this as parents demonstrating how they value their child's education. In this case, power, authority and control all reside with the principal and, in another part of the interview, s(he) emphasize that s(he) is accountable to the educational bureaucracy, not the school council. The Assistant Principal is far better attuned to the socioeconomic realities of the 1990s, the needs of working families, the inflexibility of school function times and the narrowness of the understanding some teachers hold about the learning that takes place outside their classroom; s(he) does not have the political space to ameliorate the principal's power.

Not surprisingly, and despite the best practises of some staff, both active and silent parents feel excluded from the information flow, from decision-making processes that should involve families, and in particular, from assessment of their child's performance. An externally monitored educational audit of this school conducted soon after the research perceptively recommended, 'That the school provide information and support to the parent community regarding changes in education so that all groups are able to understand and participate in the school's future directions'.

This policy instance illustrates the importance of 'actor-preparedness' when confronted by new educational policy. This research has demonstrated how assumptions about political neutrality in sites such as the school are inappropriate. The micro-politics of educational change at the local level are far more perverse than allowed for by the state, with issues of authority and power deep-rooted and often non-negotiable. Such tensions often exclude tradeoffs.

Conclusions

Pragmatic political development requires a realignment of school and home perspectives over the nature, function, and purpose of schooling as part of each child's education. Schools, as depicted in this chapter, function just within the liberal-democratic frameworks which prioritize centralized and hierarchical structures and processes allowing devolution only for peripheral tasks. This is a barely adequate response to the complex and disparate postmodern nature of contemporary societies and the increasing importance of neighborhood and community against a weakening central state. Further decentralization to relatively autonomous and representative agencies–with more open decision making and greater teacher, parent and student participation–provides one practical and achievable way to address issues of equality of opportunity and outcome. What other institution comes close?

This chapter has established that varied, competing, and different expectations from a tableau of interest groups make school policy work complex and vulnerable to assorted inefficiencies. As a group, homes and schools need to ensure that what they do together generates a school community that feels confident in what the school is doing while building more democratic connections. This chapter has demonstrated how one cannot take it for granted that there will always be political space in which to pursue home–school issues in education policy. So far, attempts to filter power to parents have not been enough to allow the growth of a democratic eductional community.

References

AMES, C. (1993) How school-to-home communications influence parents beliefs and perceptions. *Equity and Choice*, **ix**(3), 44–49.

BALL, S. J. (1994) *Educational Reform* (Buckinghamshire: Open University Press).

BERG, G. (1993) *Steering Leadership And Activity Of The School* (Uppsala University: Research Program).

CHERRYHOLMES, C. H. (1994) More notes on pragmatism. *Educational Researcher*, **23**, 15–18.

CLEVERLEY, J. (1971) *The First Generation: School And Society In Early Australia* (Sydney: Sydney University Press).

CRUMP, S. J. (1992a) Educational policy and political reform, in T. J. Lovat (ed.), *Sociology For Teachers* (Sydney: Social Science Press), 227–238.

CRUMP, S. J. (1992b) Pragmatic policy development: problems and solutions in education. *Journal of Education Policy*, **7**, 415–125.

CRUMP, S. J. (1993) *School-Centred Leadership: Putting Policy Into Practice* (Melbourne: Thomas Nelson).

CRUMP, S. J. (1995) Toward action and power: post-enlightenment pragmatism? *Discourse*, **16**, 203–218.

CRUMP, S. J. and ELTIS, K. J. (1995a) School–home connections: political relations in policy implementation. Paper presented to the Annual Meeting of the American Educational Research Asssociation, San Francisco, April.

CRUMP, S. J. and ELTIS, K. J. (1995b) School–home links in Baysview community. Paper presented to the Seventh Annual International Roundtable on Families, Communities, Schools and Children's Learning, San Francisco Press Club, San Francisco, 17 April 1995.

CUTTANCE, P. (1993) *Quality Assurance: Review Report* (Sydney: NSWDSE).

EVERS, C. W. (1993) Analytic and post-analytic philosophy of education: methodological reflections. *Discourse*, **13**, 35–45.

FRUTCHER, N., GALLETTA, A. and WHITE, J. L. (1993) New directions in parent involvement. *Equity and Choice*, **9**(3), 33–43.

GARRISON, J. (1994) Realism, Deweyan pragmatism, and educational research. *Educational Researcher*, **23**, 5–14.

GEWIRTZ, S. BALL, S. J. and BOWE, R. (1994) Parents, privilege and the education market-place. *Research Papers in Education*, **9**, 3–29.

GLENN, C. (1992) Who should own the schools? *Equity and Choice*, **9**, 59–63.

IANNACCONE, L. and LUTZ, F. W. (1995) The crucible of democracy: the local arena, in J. D. Scribner and D. H. Layton (eds), *The Study of Educational Politics* (London: Falmer Press).

JOHNSON, W. (1993) Participation means partnership. *Parent and Citizen*, **44**(3), 28–30.

MAWSON, T. (1994) Parent participation, teacher–parent practices and perceptions at an urban government primary school. Unpublished BEd (Hons) Thesis, University of Sydney.

RORTY, R. (1983) *Consequences of Pragmatism* (Minneapolis: University of Minnesota Press).

RORTY, R. (1991) *Objectivity, Relativism And Truth, Philosophical Papers*, Vol. 1 (Cambridge, MA: Cambridge University Press).

TOOMEY, D. (1996) The dark side of parent involvement in schools. *Forum*, **51**(1), in press.

WALKER, J. C. (1988) *Louts And Legends: Male Youth Culture In An Inner Urban School* (Sydney: Allen & Unwin).

WHITE, J. and WEHLAGE, G. (1995) Community collaboration: if it is such a good idea, why is it so hard to do? *Educational Evaluation and Policy Analysis*, **17**(1), 23–38.

6.   *Schools' understanding of changing communities*

Benjamin Levin and J. Anthony Riffel
University of Manitoba

Introduction

Everywhere schools feel the pressures of social change and wonder how to respond to it. In this chapter we report briefly on a study of school system efforts to think about and cope with social change, and in particular we focus on our colleagues in five school districts. We found that educators see many social changes occurring around them which they believe make the work of schooling more difficult. They lack both an analytical frame and an effective set of responses. The districts we studied have been willing and able to take some internal steps toward coping, but have not been successful in building interorganizational linkages. They are willing to accept externally imposed change, but have shown little realization that changes in families require fundamental changes in schools.

Our research

The research reported in this chapter is part of a larger study of the ways in which schools and school systems try to understand, learn about and cope with social change. Our study assumes that patterns of thought and patterns of action are related, and that both are important to study. The research involved collaborative case studies with five school districts in a Canadian province. Participating districts included a significant inner-city urban district, a suburban district, a district that was both suburban and rural, a rural agricultural district and a self-governing aboriginal education authority on an Indian reserve. The districts ranged in size from 1100 to 30,000 students, and included a wide range of economic and social settings.

In each district we reviewed official documents such as Board and administrative minutes and interviewed trustees, senior administrators and school principals. In total we conducted 43 formal interviews as well as participated in various meetings and informal conversations.

Each interview sought the respondent's identification of the most important external influences facing schools. In most cases we also asked about these three issues: labour force change, child poverty, and information technology. Written records of each interview were returned to each respondent and we incorporated respondents' amendments in the final version.

We designed the study to be collaborative and useful to our cooperating districts. To this end we wrote a case study report for each district, sent this to all our respondents in the district, and held follow-up meetings to discuss our reports and the districts' responses to them, resulting in some changes in our case reports. In this

0268–0939/97 $12 · 00 © 1997 Taylor & Francis Ltd.

chapter we refer to data from 'our colleagues in partner districts'. However, all interpretations are the responsibility of the authors, and not of our partners.

The study is rooted in an interpretivist view of organizational functioning. We
do not assume that organizations are necessarily responsive to external change in any
direct or linear way, and we are drawn to research that illuminates the ambiguities,
complexities and contradictions of life in organizations. A fuller account of the theoretical background to our work is available in Levin (1993) and Levin and Riffel
(1997).

Perceptions of changing families and communities

Many of our colleagues felt that changes in families and therefore in the children com-
ing into the schools were the most important changes facing schools. The dominant
sentiment was that families were no longer as strong as they once were and that the
importance of other institutions such as churches had also declined.

> The family is not the same as it used to be and the influence that parents had on the children doesn't seem to be what it used
> to be. Perhaps that is because both parents are working outside of the home, and there is less family being conducted in the
> home. At the same time, the churches are less influential on families than they used to be, and they have little relevance for
> young people. (Urban district superintendent)

Perceived problems in families lead to a view that schools face more problems. One
frequently cited example involved increasing numbers of children who are violent,

> I would say that the incidence is increasing. We're hearing about that from all areas. We are hearing about it from teachers
> constantly, we're hearing about it from parents whose children are in classrooms with behaviourally challenging children.
> We're seeing it reflected in the number of incidents that are reported regularly to the board by the superintendent. What is,
> I think, striking, is that those incidents of violence, of aggression, of behaviour that we would consider out of the ordinary
> or unusual are happening in younger and younger children. (Suburban district board member)

More young people in high school are living on their own.

> We do certainly have many of our students living on their own at the age of 16, 17 or 18. They work part-time, study part-
> time, and really live in a very difficult situation. (Urban district principal)

In all these situations, parents are seen as either less able or less willing to provide support and direction to their children.

> The family unit is no longer the father and the mother and the children with the dad and mom working and all coming
> home at five o'clock to get together and share the day's events. It is not a common factor in our community any longer. I
> do not have the percentages at my fingertips. I do know that in one of our elementary feeder schools the number of single
> parent families is 60%...I suspect that the number of single parent families in our own school would be between 40 and
> 50%. That has had a major impact on our students...we have a lot of students in our school who are coming in our doors
> the first thing in the morning very much stressed as a result of having to look after younger siblings, working to keep the
> family going, sharing crowded conditions with little, if any, study area opportunity to work on their work, and as a result
> of abuse through neglect which forces many of our kids to be much older than their years. I am finding that this is becoming
> more and more of a common thread amongst our student population. (Suburban and rural district principal)

As a result, eduators feel themselves under pressure to provide more and different services.

> I think it is due to the social situation here, the economic situation. There is really poor housing, there is no employment.
> That's what I think it is. Also, sometimes somebody will say: 'My child is not going to school today because they have no
> lunch'. So we try to provide lunch here for them–to help the kids. (Aboriginal district board member)

Our colleagues tend to see these services as necessary in order to meet the pressing
needs of students, but also feel that they stretch the mandate of the school.

The public demands are sometimes inconsistent, but some of that is also our responsibility. Who was at the forefront of initi-
ating life skills education? Mainsteaming education? Promoting technology? Feeding hungry children? I look at it this
way: there are sufficient numbers of us in education who are so dedicated to the welfare of the child that we are prepared
to accept responsibility that goes beyond education We feel it's our obligation to do the parenting if no one else is doing it.
If the child is going to go home where there are no adults present, we feel that it's our responsibility to care for that child during those hours. But no one gives us money to do these things. We are as responsible as the public for adding to our mana-
date. I believe that these initiatives are probably a measure of how far teachers' professional compassion goes, but there are
some consequences to assuming these responsibilities. (Suburban district superintendent)

Though our colleages recognize the importance of this role, they are also ambivalent
about it, often feeling that the social responsibilities of the school are distracting
from its primary academic purpose.

I do not think the schools can do any more than they are doing. We often put the basic education on the back burner for a
while and a lot of this stuff that we are trying to do preventive work for creeps in. I do not think it is right that we have to
spend so much time in the school trying to solve all the problems that have happened outside of the school. That is exactly
what we are faced with. (Rural district principal)

In short, the educators with whom we worked saw changes in families and communities as having major consequences for the schools, most of which made their work
more difficult.

Limits to understanding

Several points seem particularly important about these views and the way they are
formed. First, our colleagues' sense of how their communities are changing is rooted
in their direct contact with students, or the reports of other professionals on their
direct contact with students. Personal experience, direct or indirect, is the key way
people form their sense of what is happening. Individual incidents take on great sal-
ience even if they are quite unusual. The few cases, for example, of quite violent children occupy a great deal of time and energy, and hence have a powerful influence
on the way people think about the entire context of schooling.

Organized attempts to understand and think about issues of community changes
were infrequent. Though our colleagues realize that social change is having important
impacts on their work, they do not devote much time or attention to collecting data
about change or to thinking through its nature and implications. We found few men-
tions in such documents as school board minutes or administrative team minutes of
larger social issues; these fora were dominated in most settings by day-to-day administrative issues or by instructional questions such as curriculum or evaluation changes.
Similarly, professional development activities are rarely linked to the world outside
the school, focusing also on instructional issues. Few of our colleagues referred in the
interviews to organized data collection or research as helping to shape perceptions,
even though at least one of the districts did gather and distribute such data. Talk
tended to be of how change was getting in the way of the normal or traditional
tasks of the school, even though many of our colleagues recognized that there were
problems in this perspective.

We spend quite a bit of time meeting to discuss how we are going to accomplish what we have to do over the next few
weeks. We spend time on how board policy and finances will impact on the district. We do spend a lot of time on managing
the system. What we don't spend enough time on is the vision for the system, where we are going, how what I'm doing
affects what other districts are doing. It would take a more concerted effort from all of us here to set aside some of the
time that gets spent in management issues and put it into long-term planning. (Urban district superintendent)

Many of our colleagues have a notion of the ideal family, in educational terms. They seem to believe that what works for middle-class or traditional families should work for everybody. None of the districts had begun to actively question these assumptions.

Our colleagues tended to express their concerns in terms of individuals rather than larger social processes. We heard very few comments about overall changes in social and economic structures that might be leading to the kinds of problems schools were facing. Where such comments were made, they tended to be rather general. For example:

> I strongly believe that a number of societal factors have caused an increase in dysfunctional families. We have one family that recently lost their home due to excessive gambling. . . They have moved into this area with a vengeance. We have an alcoholism problem, and we have a high unemployment rate in some areas. Our northern stretch traditionally has high unemployment, and there's a sense of hopelessness there. We have a number of single parents struggling to raise families as well. We also have a high aboriginal population in this district. (Rural and suburban district administrator)

We felt in these districts a disjuncture between problem and attention. One would expect that an organization seeing itself facing a major set of problems would invest some time and energy in investigating these problems in order to understand their dimensions and to be in a better position to formulate responses. Such does not seem to be the case in regard to our partner districts and the issues of family and community change. Although these issues are seen as important and as problematic, we found little evidence that any of the districts invested commensurate resources in learning about and thinking about these changes, their implications for schools, and the ways in which schools might better respond.

Strategies and solutions

Given an individualist orientation to the problems, schools have tended to adopt individualist strategies for coping. Efforts centre on working with students so that they can manage in the traditional school programme. For the most part these take two forms: adding new services to cope directly with identified needs, and extending traditional services to deal with different kinds of problems.

In the former category we place initiatives such as meal programmes for students, the distribution of warm winter clothing, or the creation of housing registries to try to reduce family mobility. A number of schools and districts had such programmes, especially in the inner-city area of the urban district and in the aboriginal district. These programmes embodied the belief that the regular academic activities would not work unless supplemented with programmes to meet basic social needs.

> Research studies identify primary needs and demonstrate that it is difficult to focus on secondary needs until you satisfy the primary need. Consequently it is very difficult for students here to focus on education needs when in fact they do not know where they will be living the next day, and when they will be eating. (Urban district principal).

Activities such as extended use of guidance counsellors, special classes for violent students, revised school conduct codes, adding curriculum content on nutrition, and so on we regard as examples of extending traditional services. Here the schools are trying to use existing methods to cope with new problems.

> The board supports a breakfast programme at [one] school, and has also provided extra staff, a full time guidance counsellor and a resource teacher, so there has been some input where it is needed. . .At [another school] where I was previously, we had a full time resource teacher, a full time guidance counsellor, and we also had a community liaison worker, and, through a grant from the government we had a staff person who would work with students who needed extra help. Many of those

students came from low income backgrounds and many were experiencing social problems in the home. The staff person would visit the homes in August and ensure that the students had the supplies and clothing necessary to start school in September. (Suburban/rural district principal)

Schools were trying to work with other social agencies to assist students and families, but found these efforts frustrating.

What we want is for the various agencies in town. . .to work together and to approach these individuals as a unit. As a school we have gotten these people together twice now because it is a community concern. The individual has to be dealt with and we must provide the supports. But unfortunately, every one says 'Confidentiality! We cannot share any information with you. We will listen to what you have to say but we can't share anything with you.' So there are two people who are willing to talk but another eight who say that they cannot reveal anything to anybody else. . .As a result we are working at cross-purposes rather than working together for economy of resources and the best interests of the kid and the community. (Rural district principal)

These strategies were seen as add-on-programmes or special projects. They depended largely on the initiative and energy of individuals rather than on systemic practises and policies. During the time of our study, cuts in provincial government funding were forcing difficult choices on districts, and many of these supplementary programmes were seen as vulnerable; the core function of the school continues to be seen as teaching the formal curriculum.

Some respondents did suggest that the nature and scale of social change required a more fundamental shift in approach by schools.

We are now in a post-industrial society with all kinds of different needs. Employment is not guaranteed any more, society is no longer able to meet its obligations to those who are less able, financial resources are dwindling, and technology is impacting our daily lives in numerous ways. The public school system has a mandate to continue what it has always done, but I think it will be unable to do this without being totally restructured, and without having the community try and have some vision of the type of education it wants for the future generation. (Urban district principal)

Still, this perspective was less common than the view that saw changes in families as undermining the real work of the school. Almost all the official work of districts remained within the traditional frame of schooling, in which academic work around the formal curriculum remains the key task and everything else is subordinated to that work. Even as our colleagues point out how much more difficult and less relevant this task is becoming, most remain committed to it as the centre of their institution's role.

What might be done?

Although we are critical of the lack of sustained attention that school districts appear to be giving to social change, we also recognize the barriers to do otherwise. We acknowledge the moral problem of academics who, removed from the setting, sit in judgment on those struggling every day with formidable challenges. Our colleagues in the five districts are committed educators, working hard–very, very hard in many cases–for the welfare of their students. Many of them feel real anguish about the situations of their students. Our colleagues often feel overwhelmed by the problems they face and the limited resources they can bring to bear to meet them. On top of all this, districts are recipients of a flow of new government mandates that seem to them to be distractions from the real problems. We would not want anything in this account to be read as denigrating or belittling our colleagues' motivation or efforts.

Many theorists have noted the powerful influence of traditional practise, the focus on business-as-usual that dominates organizations, and the difficulty organizations have in imagining their future as being very different from their past (e.g. March 1984, 1991, Dror 1986, March and Olsen 1989, Wilson 1989, Lindblom 1990). Working on learning organizations (e.g. Daft and Huber 1987, Levitt and March 1988, Dogson 1993, Robinson 1995), though it has some important implications, often takes too little account of the realities of life in most organizations, and especially in public organizations today as they confront increasing expectations, diversifying demands, and shrinking resources.

Nonetheless, we do think it is possible to do better, even with all the limitations. We suggest that schools and school systems try four strategies:

1. *Change people's base of information.* Though personal experience will always remain potent, school systems might look at ways of introducing more diverse sources of information about changes in families and communities. Analytical information, such as census or other data on demographics, is one potential source. Looking for external commentary that is relevant is another. For example, many educators see single-parent families as a problem, even though the evidence suggests that once income level is controlled (poverty rates are very high for single female parents), having one parent or two accounts for little variation in educational outcomes (Levin 1994, Grissmer *et al.* 1994).

   But textual information will not be enough. We also need to look at changing personal interactions. If we were to create more direct contact between educators and community members we could create fuller understandings of communities and better dialogue about the needs and aspirations of people outside the school. As one respondent suggested to us, 'If you want to change what people think, change who they have lunch with'.

2. *Create some dialogue and discussion in the organization about this issue.* Educators are uncertain about the nature and implications of changes in families and communities. People need to talk about these issues, exchange points of view, consider options, and think through possibilities. In the absence of these opportunities viewpoints and actions will rest on slogans, not thought. Discussion of community context and change should be part of school board meetings, administrators' meetings, staff meetings, student council meetings, parent–teacher gatherings, and any other forum where people discuss education policy and practise.

3. *Try a wider range of strategies.* Our data suggest that schools have focused on a relatively small number of strategies in trying to cope with changing communities. The strategies being used all seem reasonable ones, but there are many other possibilities that might be considered, including reallocating staff, changing the use of facilities, changing curricula, working more directly with parents and with community organizations, and so on.

4. *Move beyond thinking primarily about individual programmes.* The relationship between schools and their communities is a complex one. Changes in families and communities are such that schools' traditional strategies are less and less adequate. Schools will need to consider a strategic response to this issue that involves not only some specific programmes for some selected students, but that involves the changes in the overall curriculum of the school, the training and professional development of staff, the way in which the school organizes and timetables, and especially in relation to other groups

and organizations. We will need to reconsider the whole idea of what schooling is.

Key to all of these strategies is an attitude that values imagination, experimentation, and learning. Since we are still far from a good understanding of relationships between schools and communities and since both schools and communities are changing as we go, we have to try many different approaches and assess their merits. The strategies might look quite different in different systems. The local, social, and political context must be a consideration in thinking about how one can address social change more systematically and effectively. But we believe that even in the midst of all the problems and challenges we can and must do more to understand and respond to changing communities.

References

DAFT, R. and HUBER, G. (1987) How organizations learn, in N. DiTomaso and S. Bacharach (eds), *Research in the Sociology of Organization*, Vol. 5 (Greenwich, CT: JAI Press).

DODGSON, M. (1993) Organizational learning: a review of some literatures. *Organizational Studies*, **14**(3), 375–394.

DROR, Y. (1986) *Policymaking Under Adversity* (New York: Transaction Books).

GRISSMER, D., KIRBY, S., BERENDS, M. and WILLIAMSON, S. (1994) *Student Achievement And The Changing American Family* (Santa Monica, CA: Rand Corporation).

HEDBERG, B. (1981) How organizations learn and unlearn, in P. Nystrom and W. Starbuck (eds), *Handbook of Organizational Design* (New York: Oxford University Press), 3–28.

LEVIN, B. (1993) School response to a changing environment. *Journal of Administration*, **31**(2), 4–21.

LEVIN, B. (1994) Education looks at poverty: conceptions and misconceptions. In S. Lawton, E. Tanenzapf and R. Townsend (eds), *Education and Community* (Toronto: OISE).

LEVIN, B. and RIFFEL, J. A. (1997) School system responses to external change: implications for parental choice of schools. In R. Glatter, P. Woods and C. Bagley (eds), *Parent Choice of Schools* (London: Routledge).

LEVITT, B. and MARCH, J. (1988) Organizational learning. *Annual Review of Sociology*, **14**, 319–340.

LINDBLOM, C. (1990) *Inquiry And Change* (New Haven, CT: Yale University Press).

MARCH, J. (1984) How we talk and how we act: administrative theory and administrative life, in T. Sergiovanni and J. Corbally (eds), *Leadership and Organizational Culture* (Urbana, IL: University of Illinois Press), 18–35.

MARCH, J. (1991) Exploration and exploitation in education. *Organizational Science*, **2**(1), 71–87.

MARCH, J. and OLSEN, J. (1989) *Rediscovering Institutions* (New York: Free Press).

ROBINSON, V. (1995) Organizational learning as organizational problem-solving. *Leading and Managing*. **1**(1), 63–78.

WILSON, J. (1989) *Bureaucracy* (New York: Basic Books).

Part 3

7. Fundamentalists, social capital, and children's welfare: a place for religion in public education?

Duane Covrig
University of California, Riverside

Introduction

Recently, *Vanity Fair* dubbed Walt Disney's Michael Eisner one of the world's most influential individuals, claiming that 'of the three seeming universal institutions–church, state, and Disney–Eisner heads the only one that could possibly launch a children's crusade today' (September 5, 1995), a painful assessment indicative that institutions other than home, church, or state have captured children's attentions. For example, Hollywood and Wall Street have carved out an influential role in children's lives due more to selfish interest than social concern. While the crusade-producing power of the church, the state (specifically public schools), and the family may be lacking, these institutions still provide the basic building blocks for children's moral, academic and social identities and they do it with children's well-being at heart.

Secularization and urbanization have helped fragment relationships among church, public school, and family. Previously, these three institutions enjoined strong overlapping influences in the lives of children (see Tyack and Hansot 1982, Lowe 1986, Reese 1992). These three institutions created a strong force against unbridled individualism (see Bellah *et al.* 1985, 1991). However, rapid movement away from smaller neighborhood social structures, increased commercialism, entertainment, and other social and legal forces have led to a greater fragmentation of communities (Scott and Meyer 1991).

Different solutions have emerged in response to this fragmentation. The growth of private schools is one response to these changes. Private schools provide parents an opportunity to reconstruct their own communities as protection from social and moral fragmentation. Church membership is another means to modifying fragmentation. Children with strong religious family and personal values can attend public schools for their exposure to public norms and church for their religious values.

Both fundamentalists and communitarians choose the path of resisting fragmentation. Both seek community development. Communitarians seek a great society built on republican values, recognizing specific roles for church and family (Selznick 1992). Fundamentalists cite a religious heritage in US history as a basis for community building. For them revelation and God scripture the values of community. In this paper I focus on fundamentalism.

While Provenzo (1990) provides an excellent review of fundamentalists' ideological conflict with public schools, our focus here is to capture the essence of their concerns. Lawrence (1989) masterfully explores fundamentalism as a 'religious ideology

0268–0939/97 $12 · 00 © 1997 Taylor & Francis Ltd.

of protest' (p. 83) against modernism which ironically uses politics, a modern-age tool. Politics provides a channel for the fundamentalists' desire to reinfuse religious values in public life. The public school board is accessible and attached to schools, a value-laden social-political institution. This chapter reflects on fundamentalist concerns. In the first three sections, social capital theory establishes the legitimacy of fundamentalists' concerns about alternative values for schools and communities. Also, I explore two alternatives for allowing religion a place in public education. I conclude with a personal note.

Social capital

Before his death, Coleman (1988, 1990a, 1990b) used social capital to underscore how people make choices that preserve their utilitarian interests but that 'are shaped, re-directed, [and] constrained by the social context [like] norm, interpersonal trust, social networks, and social organization' (1988: s96). 'Social capital...is not a single entity but a variety of different entities, with two elements in common: they all consist of some aspect of social structures and they facilitate certain action of actors − whether persons or corporate actors − within the structure' (p. s98). Social capital is less tangible than other forms of capital, like physical or human capital, because 'it exists in the *relations* among persons' (pp. s100, 101). It provides the guiding force which socializes individuals and provides resources for building human capital.

This theory is useful for thinking about children's welfare. It suggests that social structures between parent and teacher provide for the reinforcement of values and the development of human capital. Shared values enhance children's development.

Certain ways of organizing both within and outside schools promise to provide stronger reinforcing influences on children which may promote more stable development. Zucker (1991) reminds us that some of the strongest and most persistent institutional influences are those we take for granted. 'Social knowledge once institutionalized as a fact, as part of the objective reality...can be transmitted directly on that basis' and 'the moral becomes factual' (p. 83).

Some schools have strong reinforcing social structures that exert a more powerful influence on children. There is a strong sense of 'the way we do things around here.' Such environments offer a degree of security to children (and adults as well). This helps to limit uncertainty and overcome some of the limitations of rational processing (Simon 1976, Guy 1990). Other schools have self-defeating practices that do not present a united 'ethos' for students. Furthermore, each child may respond to the same practices differently because of their experiences with other community structures. Cusick (1973) documented the influence of peer groups, but two other influences are church and home. The combined influence of a reinforcing school, church and home life may have a multiplicative effect on developing rich social capital for children.

This explanation of social capital expands Coleman's social network ideas. Each child lives in a community and operates in several different groups simultaneously (Selznick 1992: 357–417, 1994). Some children have access to community structures that tightly constrain and focus development and contribute to academic performance (see Coleman *et al.* 1982). However, other children experience conflicting social influences making development problematic. What measures reduce inequities of social capital among children?

Fundamentalism as a concern about social capital

Social capital theory may be used to enlighten the fundamentalist argument. Fundamentalists perceive a disparity between their home–church values and those fostered at public schools. When the key actors in a child's community do not actively reinforce a particular value there is a decrease in the multiplicative support of that value. As a result, that value may disappear or at least become minimized in the child's available social capital. If that value is important, its decrease indicates an impoverishment. Concern for children led fundamentalists to view these disparities as erosions to social capital.

Disagreement about values depletes social capital. As a child experiences disagreement, s/he may conclude that no adequate authority guides personal development. Important issues may come to be seen as matters of preference. Children develop a feeling that 'I am on my own' in these matters. This is unfortunate because children need more direction than a teeming cacophony of ideas. They need social input, guidance and even sanctioning in order to develop. They need to be cared for, in Mayeroff's sense (1971). Such care seeks development in the other.

Fundamentalists do not hold a monopoly of concern over erosion of social capital. Critics of fundamentalism also worry about this. They also fear that some values will be reinforced that shouldn't be a part of social capital. For example, racist tendencies fostered in a small community may run against national values of equality and tolerance. Children reared in such a community may realize only later, or not at all, that racism is antagonistic to the moral ideas of the larger community.

Fundamentalists resist forces that threaten their values. They attempt to protect key values within the available social capital. Therefore, fundamentalists' resistance may be seen as a crusade against destructive forces threatening children. Like many educators who claim moral high ground in defending children's welfare through resisting ignorance, social abandonment of children, and encroachment on school funding, fundamentalists are also crusaders for children's welfare in the preservation of social capital. But tensions remain in the definition of social capital.

Whose values construct social capital?

Both parents and teachers have a mission to protect children's social capital. Dewey (1990/1900) argued that 'what the best and wisest parent wants for his own child, that must the community want for all its children' (p. 7). The problem is the wise parents disagree! However, Dewey addressed an important connection between public schools and democratic community structure. He suggested social order directs the values provided by education. First, citizens use the democratic process to derive values that are to be commonly reinforced. Second, those reinforced values are those that allow children to participate in the democratic process. 'The extent in which the interests of the group are shared by all its members, and the fullness and freedom with which' interaction takes place characterizes democracy (Dewey 1966/1916: 99). So, education must prepare individuals to have a 'personal interest in social relationships and control, and the habits of mind which secure social changes without introducing disorder' (Dewey 1966/1916: 99). For Dewey, democracy dictates requirements for important values. These dynamic democratic values are not static values of religious authority. 'An undesirable society...is one which internally and externally sets up barriers to free intercourse and communication of experience' (p. 99). Dewey's words suggest that social capital rests on skills and values which stress social construction of knowledge, promote adaptability to new situations, and lead children into democratic dialogue.

Gutmann (1987) opts for democratic state education that fosters the values of nonrepression of ideas and nondiscrimination among groups. She envisions four types of educational system and rejects the first three as antagonistic to democratic values. The first, the family state, relies on too few individuals to run the state. The second, the state of families, provides too much control to families who could advance undemocratic values, such as bigotry and exclusivism. The third, the state of individuals, posits that good is determined solely by the person, but Gutmann argues that society has a pressing need for more than just individually realized good. Society needs a common good.

Spring (1994) observes that a democratic notion of finding moral truth is threatening to many religious groups who think it has already been found in revelation or sacred scripture. He notes that 'these groups might object to Gutmann's principle of nonrepression of thinking about alternatives to the good life and to Dewey's belief that truth and knowledge are products of social relationships' (p. 30) in that reconstruction opens the door to radical destruction of normative structures and traditional values. One response to Spring would be to demand that religious groups acknowledged democratic critiques inherent in free speech and democratic principles. However, the founding fathers moved toward a republican concept of government, one in which democracy held sway, but was continually checked by the right of individual and religious belief.

Spring's ideas facilitate our discussion here because they raise a necessary doubt about 'natural' freedom and value in democracy. Are democratic values necessarily the values the wisest parents would want for their children? The idea that wholesale acceptance of tolerance and moral pluralism will ensure a democratic, morally stable society is questionable. Tolerance and discourse are necessary, but are they sufficient values in a democracy. Intolerance is not the only conceivable threat to democracy. Moral ambiguity also threatens the necessary reinforcing structures of democracies. When citizens can find no agreed upon norms to direct their behaviours is discourse enough to decrease ambiguity, establish a wholesome sense of moral authority, and foster a sense of community commitment?

I am reminded of two descriptions for 'hell.' Some have argued that 'hell' is any place with no doors, where no sharing, no learning and no development can take place. This is a totalitarian hell in which ideas are repressed. This is the hell that Gutmann fears. It arises when the principles of nondiscrimination and nonrepression are continually violated. This is a real hell. History is full of examples of such places. Newspaper headlines still remind us of their existence. Democracy was formed to eliminate such hells. Democratic education was conceived to direct students away from totalitarian thinking.

However, 'hell' also can be conceived of as a place with nothing but doors, where no walls protect the social life within. Limits, moral and political, boundaries, borders and walls, both self-defined and community supported, are crucial for the development of children. While walls connote elitism, separateness, and oppressive social exclusivism, they also depict protection from unwanted forces that tyrannize the moral tenderness of children. Bellah et al. (1985) remind us that 'freedom only takes on its real meaning in a certain kind of society, with a certain form of life. Without that, Jefferson saw freedom as quickly destroying itself and eventuating in tyranny' (p. 31). Bellah *et al.* further argue that 'mass society of mutually antagonistic individuals' is 'easy prey to despotism' (p. 38). Regretfully, the modern person is more rooted in personal rights than in a biblical or even a republican concept of society (p. 143). While Gutmann's ideas promise to protect against destructive individualism through dialogue, something more than dialogue has to exist. Maguire and Fargnoli (1991) proposed a 'fundamental moral experience' to foster deep respect for others. They argue compellingly that religious experience has done much to nourish the 'fundamental moral experience' through its narratives. The Judeo-Christian narratives which fundmentalists promote can be a profound vehicle for fostering respect for others.

Toward practical solutions

So far, this paper has raised more questions than answers. I now turn to a practical discussion of religion in public education. Those interested in a comprehensive and extremely thorough discussion of the alternatives should read Nord's (1995) daunting treatise on this topic. I have confined my discussion to Noddings's (1993) cognitive-pedagogical solution and Holmes's (1992) structural solution.

Noddings (1993) opts for 'pedagogical neutrality...in discussing religious questions' (p. 133) but thinks teachers should seek an 'education for intelligent belief or unbelief [that] is as much education of the heart as it is...of the mind' (p. xiv). Both planned and spontaneous dialogue about the contributions of religion to social life and the development of existential meaning can help students explore important values. The natural inquiry of students and the context and content of the curriculum allow the empathetic teacher a forum to explore values attached to the basic meanings of life, death, evil, good, and God. She wants teachers and students to engage in critical analysis.

Noddings pushes the issue of religion in public education past a 'comparative-religions' approach to a more existential and dynamic exploration of meaning. This is done while avoiding the 'evils' of proselytizing. Nevertheless, for all her concern about facilitating emotive experiences through religion, her approach is not much more than a comparative religions approach with a greater degree of pedagogical spontaneity.

This approach cannot begin to capture the contributions (negative and positive) which membership in a religious community makes to the social capital of children. This is evident in her discussion of 'belonging.' She acknowledged that joining a church was 'not necessarily unintelligent...[but] a form of practical or instrumental intelligence' (p. 42). While it is the 'reflective intelligence that we hope to encourage in our attempts to educate' (p. 42) the instrumental belonging in community may be one of the central elements by which 'the connection between humans and divinity...[and] the deepest metaphysical and existential questions are engaged' (p. 42). Regretfully, 'belonging' to a religious community is not achieved in public schools or through Noddings's approach.

Fundamentalists could critique Noddings's approach to religion as nice but facile because it is not grounded in practice. The separation of religious discussion from religious practice could be argued as similar to the separation of theory from practice, an evil a Deweyan scholar like Noddings might be expected to avoid.

Fundamentalists could argue that this cognitive emphasis does little to offer children the motivational, inspirational, and emotional substances that religion brings to life. In church, myths are not merely analyzed but experienced; ritual is not merely discussed and memorized but apprehended. It is experience that gives meaning and provides and promotes strong community ties. However, Noddings' thesis captures the essence of religious discourse by tying it to the existential questions that emerge from students' experiences.

Noddings's ideas at least open the public school door to the discussion of religion, but fundamentalists are likely to question the potential excesses of full and open dialogue. They may wish to have greater control of the substance of these discussions as a way of managing any moral or religious ambiguity that may develop. Is it enough to say *caveat emptor* and neutrally dispense facts about religion to young minds? Holmes's (1992) community schools might allow parents more control over the marketplace of ideas.

Holmes (1992) addresses the problems a highly pluralistic society provides for the integrative processes of schooling. He uses the idea of decentralization and choice to suggest that the notion of the common school is no longer viable in our heterogeneous Western democracies. Common schools 'face the combined challenges of fundamental dissent about ideology and purpose, and social, religious and cultural heterogeneity represented by pluralism and multiculturalism' (p. vi). He does not think public schools can assimilate and integrate this diversity yet fears that abandonment of the concept of 'public' education is equally detrimental. Holmes attempts to charter a third way through these two extremes by arguing for publicly funded schools which meet the needs of communities whose borders are not so much geographic as ideological, moral, social and religous (p. 15). He notes that 'the problem is less that we disagree about education, than that we have come to believe we ought to agree' (p. 1).

Holmes advances four options for dealing with a highly pluralistic society. First, he proposes sustaining common schools by building primarily on the values of equity and efficiency. Holmes calls this a low doctrine of public schools. In trying to be inclusive it fails to focus school resources on shared values. Overall, he dismisses this option because it excludes many disssenting values, specifically religious ones. The second option encourages the development of diverse programs and schools within the public school system. Diversifying the type of schools in public education increases the potential that parents will find a place that matches their values. The third option is that public and private funding mixes to allow public and private school systems to exist. Finally, voucher initiatives can allow public funding to extend to all types of schools.

Despite Holmes's rejection of the first option, and fear of the fourth, it seems that he is looking for a restructuring from somewhere between options two and three. Finding a place for religion in public education requires restructuring and not a mere pedagogical glossing.

While I see merit in both Noddings's and Holmes's ideas, it is unclear to me which best serves children's welfare. My desire to see religion influence the social capital of children leads me to think that active participation in a Holmesian 'tight' value community is more preferable to Noddings's approach. However, Noddings's solution offers a dynamic forum in which the religious questions of children can be encouraged while religious tolerance is furthered. Making space for religion in the public schools is clearly problematic.

A concluding personal note

I conclude with a personal reflection about my own experience with religion and public education. I am an active Christian and teach Christian bioethics. As a Seventh-day Adventist (SDA) my religious development has a fundamentalist element. SDAs operate the largest Protestant K–12 school system in the USA, ostensibly as a way of preserving their religious heritage. Strong fundamentalist ideologies operate at the periphery of SDA and generate 'offshoot' movements. For example, many of the people who died in the Waco, Texas Branch Davidian compound had some connections to or had been Seventh-day Adventists. Although my heritage is fundamentalist, I am a product of the California public school system. I experienced and enjoyed the marketplace of ideas it provided me. Furthermore, SDAs' active participation in health care and higher education has created a strong appreciation for advanced learning within our membership. So in my own community, Biblical literalism is continually tempered by reason and science. Furthermore, SDAs have elevated the belief in separation of church and state beyond good politics to good religion. A widespread acceptance of the separation doctrine is evident in our church's eschatological beliefs. Church tradition has argued that one of the biggest threats to our faith and practice will eventually come from religious zealots who want their religious practices forced on others. For that reason, encroachments on the separation of church and state are promptly resisted by SDA official statements and even church-sponsored court action. We often sound more like the American Civil Liberty Union than Protestants.

For these reasons, I foster a disdain for fundamentalist tactics which smack of religious tyranny but sympathize with their belief that religious ideas strengthen communities. I am still looking for a solution to these conflicting feelings. I believe I am not alone. The idea of social capital provides a vehicle for me to think about 'fundamentalist' concerns. However irritating and potentially detrimental fundamentalist disregard for tolerance can be, I sense their interest in the welfare of children. A hell with no doors, as well as a hell with no walls, threatens our chilren's welfare and our future. Thus, I keep searching, personally and academically, for a solution. In the meantime, I am committed to the challenge of listening to fundamentalists, not only for the sake of more accurately criticizing their ideas, but also in the hope that their ideas and genuine concern for children may inspire my own thinking. After all, with the welfare of children at stake, this hardly seems an impossible challenge.

References

BELLAH, R., MADSEN, R., SULLIVAN, W., SWINDLER, A. and TIPTON, S. (1985) *Habits of the Heart: Individualism and Commitment in American Life* (New York: Harper & Row).

BELLAH, R., MADSEN, R., SULLIVAN, W., SWINDLER, A. and TIPTON, S. (1991) *The Good Society* (New York: Alfred A. Knopf).

COLEMAN, J. S. (1988) Social capital in the creation of human capital. *American Journal of Sociology,* 94 (Supplement), s95–s120.

COLEMAN, J. S. (1990a) Commentary: social institutions and social theory. *American Sociological Review,* 55 (June), 333–339.

COLEMAN, J. S. (1990b) *The Foundations of Social Theory* (Cambridge, MA: Harvard University Press).

COLEMAN, J. S., HOFFER, T. and KILGOR, S. (1982) *High School Achievement: Public, Catholic, and Private Schools Compared* (New York: Basic Books).

DEWEY, J. (1990/1900) *The School and Society/The Child and the Curriculum* (Chicago: University of Chicago Press).

DEWEY, J. (1966/1916) *Democracy and Education* (New York: Free Press).

GUTMANN, A. (1987) *Democratic Education* (Princeton: Princeton University Press).

GUY, M. E. (1990) *Ethical Decision Making in Everyday Work Situations* (New York: Quorum Books).

HOLMES, M. (1992) *Educational Policy for the Pluralist Democracy: the Common School, Choice and Diversity* (Washington DC: Falmer Press).

LAWRENCE, B. (1989) *Defenders of God: the Fundamentalist Revolt against the Modern Age* (San Francisco: Harper & Row).

LOWE, J., JR (1986) Church-state issues in education: the Colonial pattern and the nineteenth century to 1870. In J. F. Wilson (ed.), *Church and State in America: A Bibliographical Guide The Colonial and Early National Periods* (New York: Greenwood).

MAGUIRE, D. C. and FARGNOLI, A. N. (1991) *On Moral Grounds: the Art/Science of Ethics* (New York: Crossroad).

MAYEROFF, M. (1971) *On Caring* (New York: Harper & Row).

NODDINGS, N. (1993) *Educating for Intelligent Belief or Unbelief* (New York: Teachers College Press).

NORD, W. A. (1995) *Religion and American Education: Rethinking a National Dilemma* (Chapel Hill, NC: University of North Carolina Press).

PROVENZO, E. (1990) *Religious Fundamentalism and American Education: the Battle for the Public Schools* (Albany, NY: State University of New York Press).

REESE, W. (1992) 'Facing the third millenium: evangelical Christians and public schools,' in *The Challenge of Pluralism: Education, Politics, and Values* (Notre Dame, IN: University of Notre Dame Press), 103–116.

SCOTT, R. and MEYER, J. (1991) The organization of societal sectors: propositions and early evidence. In W. W. Powell and P. J. DiMaggio (eds) *The New Institutionalism in Organizational Analysis* (Chicago: University of Chicago Press), 108–140.

SELZNICK, P. (1992) *The Moral Commonwealth: Social Theory and the Promise of Community* (Berkeley, CA: University of California Press).

SELZNICK, P. (1994) Thinking about community: ten theses. *Society*, 32(5), 33–37.

SIMON, H. A. (1976) *Administrative Behaviour: A study of Decision-making Processes in Administrative Organization*. 3rd edn (New York: Free Press)

SPRING, J. (1994) *Wheels in the Head: Educational Philosophies of Authority, Freedom, and Culture from Socrates to Paulo Freire* (New York: McGraw-Hill).

TYACK, D. and HANSOT, E. (1982) *Managers of Virtue: Public School Leadership in America, 1820–1980* (New York: Basic).

ZUCKER, L. (1991) The role of institutionalization in cultural persistence, in W. W. Powell and P. J. DiMaggio (eds), *The New Institutionalism in Organizational Analysis* (Chicago: University of Chicago Press), 83–107.

8.   *School privatization: friendly or hostile takeover?*

Martha McCarthy
Indiana University

> Our society is a balancing act betwen individual liberty and societal well being, freedom and oppression, and profiting and profiteering. (McLaughlin 1992: 30)

In a nation committed to free enterprise and an entrepreneurial spirit, privatization is an appealing education reform vehicle. However, a tension often exists between education's dual purposes of enhancing individual well-being and ensuring an educated citizenry essential in a democracy. Some options to increase private investment in education, such as unregulated voucher plans, favor individual interests over collective concerns. Other options, such as public school contracts with companies for targeted instruction, retain public control and accountability. This chapter reviews three strategies of private involvement in education, cites lessons learned, and illuminates value conflicts surfaced by the school privatization movement.

Voucher systems

> Full-scale choice. . .remains the linchpin of sound education reform (Bennett 1992: 65).

Most operational school choice plans involve only public schools (e.g. intradistrict or interdistrict open enrollment, magnet schools), but emerging proposals open public education to market forces. These proposals usually entail government vouchers of a specified monetary amount that parents can redeem at public or private schools.

The arguments made by advocates and critics of voucher plans have received considerable attention and will not be recounted here. In short, proponents contend that under marketplace models inferior schools would be eliminated through natural selection. They also argue that a competitive environment would enhance teachers' professional status and salaries and provide poor families with choices that previously only the rich have enjoyed. They assert that marketplace models would result in increased student performance, more parental involvement, more efficient use of school funds, and reduced overhead with accountability focused on the school rather than the school district (see Chubb and Moe 1990).

Critics fear that marketplace models mark the demise of the common school's democratizing function. They argue that middle-class parents would escape public education, leaving the disadvantaged and disabled in public schools. They claim that voucher systems would create governmental entanglement with religious schools and exacerbate economic and racial segregation. Many concerns over marketplace models centre around social justice and the impact of voucher systems on families who lack the interest or means to make informed choices (see Fowler 1991, Rothstein and Rasell 1993).

0268–0939/97 $12 · 00 © 1997 Taylor & Francis Ltd.

Although no state has undertaken a statewide voucher system, small school districts in several New England states have had *de facto* voucher systems for years. Instead of operating high schools, they have provided tuition grants for secondary students to attend public or private schools outside the district. The Supreme Court of Vermont held that such an arrangement did not unconstitutionally advance religion (*Campbell v. Manchester* 1994). Yet, proposals for state-supported vouchers redeemable at private schools have been soundly defeated by the electorate in California, Colorado, Oregon and Washington. In 1994 the Puerto Rico Supreme Court struck down a programme providing vouchers that low-income students could redeem in public or private schools as abridging Puerto Rico's constitutional ban on using public funds to support private education (*Associacion v. Torres* 1994).

However, interest in voucher plans recently has increased in the USA. A statewide voucher programme has been proposed in Pennsylvania, and the governors of California and Minnesota have proposed targeted voucher programmes to enable low-income or low-achieving students to enroll in nonpublic schools. About one third of the states are considering voucher proposals or tax credit packages that would use public funds to encourage enrollment in private schools (Richardson 1996).

Several school districts are experimenting with voucher plans for disadvantaged youth, under which parents can send their children to private schools through donation-supported vouchers. The Children's Educational Opportunity Foundation, founded in 1991, currently distributes more than $30 million in voucher funds to nearly 8000 students in 22 affiliate programmes located in Washington, DC, and 14 states (*School Board News* 1995).

In addition to privately funded plans, programmes in Milwaukee and Cleveland are publicly funded. Milwaukee's 1990 choice programme provides vouchers for up to 1500 low-income students to attend private, nonreligious schools. A 1995 attempt to expand the programme to religious schools has been struck down by the state judiciary (*Wisconsin v. Jackson* 1996). In contrast, a state court has upheld the Cleveland programme providing low-income parents vouchers that can be redeemed in public or private schools, including religious schools (*Gatton v. Goff* 1996).

There are too few voucher programmes currently operating in the USA to provide much evaluation data, and results have been mixed on studies of voucher systems in other countries (see Glenn 1990, Carnoy 1995). Milwaukee's state-supported programme allowing children to attend private schools is unique in operating long enough to assess its impact. A third-year evaluation indicated that families selecting private schools for their children were smaller; choice parents, especially mothers, were better educated and had higher educational expectations for their children; and choice parents spent more time with their children on education concerns (Witte *et al.* 1993). Research studies on the privately funded choice programmes in Indianapolis and San Antonio similarly have documented that families who select private education differ from those who remain in public schools in that the former are more interested and involved in their children's education (Martinez *et al.* 1994, Weinschrott and Kilgore 1996).

Although assertions abound, no hard evidence establishes that a marketplace model results in student achievement gains (Olson 1993, Rothstein and Rasell 1993). In the Milwaukee programme, reading scores increased after year one, but declined after years two and three (Witte *et al.* 1993). Preliminary achievement data also have been inconclusive on the few privately funded programmes (Martinez *et al.* 1993; Weinschrott and Kilgore 1996).

The final word on voucher systems may come from the courts. They have not yet determined whether voucher systems allowing public funds for sectarian education could survive challenges under the Establishment Clause or similar state constitutional provisions that prohibit the use of public funds for religious purposes. Some Supreme Court decisions lend support to the contention that state aid flowing to religious schools because of the private choices of parents satisfies the First Amendment (*Witters* v. *Washington Department* 1986, *Zobrest* v. *Catalina* 1993), but recently, lower courts have rendered conflicting rulings on voucher programmes involving religious schools.

Charter schools

> Over the past few years charter schools have sometimes seemed to take on the aura of a 'silver bullet' – a magical solution to a variety of problems. (Pipho 1995: 742)

Charter schools receive state funds but operate outside the requirements of the traditional public education bureaucracy on the basis of a grant authority (charter) usually from the state or local board of education, but sponsors can be other agencies (Wohlstetter and Anderson 1994). The intent is to give schools flexibility to innovate in instructional programmes by reducing operational constraints. Charter school laws vary considerably across states, but most authorize charter applications from existing public or private schools and groups/companies starting new schools. Charters usually can be renegotiated periodically, with continuation dependent on student performance.

In 1993 only two states – Minnesota and California – had passed charter school legislation. But by 1996, 25 states and the District of Columbia had laws authorizing charter schools. Initial charter school laws limited the number of charters allowed (from 20 to 100), but now six states place no cap on the number of charters granted and two other states have caps for only the first few years of the programme.

An interesting feature of a charter school is its 'hybrid' nature, resembling both private and public schools (Buechler 1996: 4). Similar to private schools, they function outside state regulations and can be operated by private entities. Although directly answerable to consumers (i.e. parents and students), who can select other schools if dissatisfied, charter schools are publicly funded, must accept all students who enroll without charge, and are accountable to a public agency.

Relatively few schools now hold charters, but interest in this concept is growing. Some contend that charter schools capitalize on the strengths of both private and public sectors, providing 'an appropriate compromise between the current public education system, with little or no market accountability, and a voucher system with little or no accountability to the public at large' (Buechler 1996: 3). Politicians view charter schools as an inexpensive reform because additional tax funds are not required. Critics, however, fear that public education will be undermined. They are concerned that charter school legislation might lead through the back door to vouchers, thus funnelling public funds into private schools (Hoff 1993).

Private contractors

The nation desperately needs new ways to conduct the business of educating the young, and entrepreneurship must be at the top of any list of reforms. (Doyle 1994: 129)

Use of private contractors in public education is not new. Private industry always has supplied school textbooks, equipment, and furniture, and for years private vendors have provided many services (e.g. transportation, maintenance, food). Several decades ago there were a few brief experiments with privately provided instructional services (performance contracting).

Private companies' current efforts to manage public schools or school districts have been extremely controversial. The experiences of Educational Alternatives Incorporated (EAI) are illustrative. After contracting to run single schools in a few districts, EAI signed a contract to manage nine Baltimore schools. The company received praise, even from President Clinton, for the improvements made in facilities of these schools (OIA 1994), but the project was plagued by disputes. The teachers' union was a severe critic of EAI's decisions to increase class size and to replace local teachers' aides with student-teacher interns. Also, city officials in Baltimore called for an investigation of EIA after student achievement gains were overstated in the press in 1993 (*School Board News* 1994), and EAI had problems with Maryland's Department of Education regarding instructional programmes for children with disabilities. With increasing strains between EAI and school district and city officials, the Baltimore school board terminated EAI's contract in 1995. Ironically, the previous spring's test results, released shortly after the contract cancellation, showed larger student achievement gains in EAI-managed schools (Walsh 1995a).

EAI's agreement to manage 32 Hartford, Connecticut schools (the largest private contract awarded by a school district) was aborted before the project got off the ground. In 1995, amid opposition from the teachers' union and some local residents, the project was scaled back to only five schools with EAI playing a consulting role in the management of the school district. Tensions escalated over EAI's financial terms, and in January 1996 the school board voted to terminate the contract (Walsh 1996c).

Although the value of EAI stock dropped dramatically after Baltimore's and Hartford's cancellations, company officials remain optimistic regarding EAI's future in the public school arena. Currently EAI is negotiating with several school districts to serve short-term consultancies. The company has learned from its setbacks in Baltimore and Hartford and now aims to establish itself in a district before assuming total management of school operations. For example, in 1996 EAI signed a contract to assist the Wappingers (New York) Central School District in its efforts to reduce costs by at least $4 million during the upcoming year (*Education Daily* 1996, Walsh 1996b).

The Edison Project, which was conceptualized by entrepreneur Chris Whittle, founder of Whittle Communications, is another example of corporate efforts in school management (McCarthy 1995). Edison schools are designed to be radically different from traditional schools (e.g. multi-age grouping, differentiated staffing, longer school day and year, curriculum centred on great works, extensive use of technology).

The Edison Project has contracted to run single schools in Colorado Springs; Boston; Mt. Clemens, Michigan; Sherman, Texas; and Wichita (McGriff 1995). The Project's promotional literature emphasizes that the company's goal is to give parents choices among educational philosophies rather than to manage school districts. The first four Edison schools began operating in the fall of 1995, so it is too soon to assess their merits.

In addition to the Edison Project and EAI, numerous other private companies have become involved in public education with contracts based on promises of improved student performances. For example, Nashville's Alternative Public Schools Inc. is managing a school in Wilkinsburg, Pennsylvania. The Minneapolis school board received considerably publicity in 1993 when it hired a local management consulting firm, Public Strategies Group (PSG), to run its schools, with the firm's president serving as superintendent (*School Board News* 1993). The district adopted an improvement agenda for 1994–95 that tied over $400,000 in incentive pay to PSG achieving various performance objectives (Graves 1995).

Other companies are seeking to provide targeted instructional services. Sylvan Learning Systems, which has 50 private tutoring centres nationwide, has signed contracts in Baltimore, Chicago, Washington, DC, and a number of other school districts to provide remedial services (Walsh 1995b). Sylvan agrees to improve students' reading and math skills within 12 months. Unlike EAI and the Edison Project, Sylvan has attracted little media attention, and teachers' unions do not see the company as a threat. Sylvan makes no school budgetary decisions; it is simply being paid to provide certain instructional services (McLaughlin 1992; *School Administrator* 1995).

The use of private contractors to deliver instruction is appealing to school boards for economic reasons. Financially strapped school districts under pressure to improve student learning often feel that they have little risk with a company that guarantees results; payment is contingent on students attaining certain performance standards.

Discussion

Private investment in education does not appear to be a fleeting fad (Walsh 1996a). In February 1996, the first Annual Education Industry Conference was held in New York City and drew several hundred education leaders and potential investors, who are eager to tap into the annual $300 billion spent on US K–12 education (Doyle 1996). A Lehman Brothers report stated that 'the education industry may replace health care in 1996 as the focus industry' (quoted in Walsh 1996a: 15). Companies, school boards, consumers, and the general citizenry all have a stake in the direction that efforts to privatize education take and should heed lessons learned from recent experiences. Also, policy makers need to understand the values undergirding various models of corporate involvement so that informed decisions can be made.

Lessons learned

Statewide voucher systems as well as private management of entire school districts face significant barriers. No statewide voucher system has been adopted, and Minneapolis is the only privately managed school district that has not been plagued by challenges.

Lessons definitely have been learned about the strength of teachers' unions in opposing voucher plans and corporate school management. Unions are well organized with sophisticated lobbying mechanisms and have worked tirelessly at considerable expense to defeat statewide voucher proposals and district-level private management of schools. Any strategy that 'threatens to displace existing workers, especially teachers, is going to be accused of union busting' (McLaughlin 1995: 10) and jeopardizing gains made through collective bargaining. The National Education Association has established a centre to fight for-profit contractors and has distributed a handbook of strategies to its local affiliates (*Education Daily* 1994).

Clearly, EAI underestimated the power of teachers' unions in opposing the company's efforts in Baltimore and Hartford. The American Federation of Teachers (1994) issued an analysis of EAI involvement in Baltimore, asserting that test scores and attendance declined in EAI schools, which allegedly received a disproportionate share of school district funds. In Wilkinsburg, Pennsylvania, the teachers' union mobilized after all former teachers were replaced in the elementary school managed by Alternative Public Schools, Inc., and the union has continued to plague the company through litigation, media campaigns, and efforts to elect school board members who oppose the contract (Ponessa 1995). Without question, unions and collective bargaining laws must be given serious consideration by companies and policy makers contemplating private involvement in public education.

Lessons also have been painfully learned about the importance of contract language. John McLaughlin, editor of the *Education Industry Report*, has urged companies to heed EAI's experiences and ensure that they are not assuming all the risks and that the contract cannot be cancelled 'at a political whim' (quoted in Walsh 1996c: 9). Also, school boards must be certain that contract terms can be implemented realistically and that privately managed schools are not unintentionally advantaged in resource allocations (AFT 1994).

Companies also are finding that despite waivers from some state regulations, they do not have as much discretion in personnel and instructional matters as some had envisioned. For example, civil rights mandates that prohibit discrimination in employment and require appropriate programmes for children with disabilities cannot be waived.

Private investors appear to have learned how difficult the managmeent of school operations can be; thus, more limited (and less controversial) contractual arrangements to provide targeted services have increasing appeal to the corporate world. Sylvan and similar companies, which are not being attacked by teachers' unions, are expanding their involvement in public education. School boards are becoming receptive to the idea that they do not have to supply all instructional services as long as they hold private vendors accountable. Providing targeted instructional services may indeed hold the greatest promise for companies to tap into the lucrative education market.

Charter schools also are flourishing, if the number of states adding legislation is an indication. President Clinton has applauded such schools, and federal funds have been earmarked to assist in starting charter schools. It is too soon to assess the hurdles these schools face, although some are already encountering difficulties in managing school budgets, especially in connection with services for special-needs students (Semple 1995). Also, opposition from teachers' unions may intensify as the number of charter schools increases. The jury is still out regarding whether such schools can successfully blend the best of the public and private sectors in enhancing educational opportunities or whether they will become *de facto* private schools.

Values in conflict

The school privatization movement has resulted in ideological clashes over concepts such as choice, competition, efficiency, and equity. Also, various options to increase private involvement have surfaced tensions between individual enhancement and the collective good. Values are clashing among educators, parents, business leaders, and policy makers, and these conflicts reflect different perspectives regarding the relationship between individual and societal interests in a democratic society.

It would be a mistake to lump all efforts to privatize education under one umbrella. As discussed previously, there is a continuum from pure market models to public–private partnerships. Although different assumptions guide the various options to increase private involvement in education, there are some values that undergird most of the models.

For example, voucher systems, private management of school districts, and private contracting for limited services all place high value on productivity and efficiency. Usually, efficiency is measured in terms of increased student learning and lower costs. Most of the private companies seeking contracts with school districts assert that they can produce more learning for less money, which entices school officials. However, critics fear that corporate concern for realizing profits may result in shortcuts that reduce the quality of services. They also fear that the educational goal of producing a better society will be subjugated to attaining higher test scores (Houston 1994).

Most, but not all, privatization models also emphasize empowering parents so they can make educational choices in line with their personal values. One of the few conclusive findings from the studies of voucher programmes operating to date is that parents are more satisfied and involved with schools they choose. Those advocating marketplace models of schooling want parents, rather than educators or policy makers, to be the primary architects of their children's education. Instead of state-prescribed values being advanced in public schools, parents could select the educational settings that correspond to their own beliefs.

A related assumption implicitly undergirding many privatization models is that homogeneity within individual schools should take precedence over diversity. Under marketplace models, social homogeneity is considered important to a school's performance because it reduces conflicts about goals (Chubb and Moe 1990). Edison Project officials want parents to have a choice so that those selecting an Edison school believe in the school's philosophy (McGriff 1995).

Another common assumption is that governmental involvement in education should be reduced because it leads to bureaucratized, ineffective schools (Chubb and Moe 1990, Doyle 1994). Buechler (1996) has observed that the various privatization strategies are designed 'to inject market forces. . .into what many perceive as an over-regulated, over-centralised public education monopoly with a strong allegiance to the status quo and no institutional incentive to improve student performance' (p. 3). Advoates of vouchers desire local school autonomy and accountability, and a central feature of most charter school legislation is a reduction of state controls. One reason charter school legislation appeals to the Edison Project is that Edison schools cannot be implemented under restrictive state regulations.

However, a reduced governmental role in education raises significant questions about the state's responsibility to protect individual rights and guarantee that all children receive an education necessary for citizenship in a democracy. The President's

Commission on Privatization (1988) cautioned that where public institutions have assumed important democratic functions, the shift toward market alternatives may threaten core values of our society. Also, a preliminary study of charter schools by the Education Commission of the States emphasized that governmental oversight is extremely important to ensure that charters are not abused by groups that might pursue discriminatory practises (*Education Week*, 1995). Does the state have a duty to ensure that all children are exposed to certain values and academic content to advance the common good, or should parents be able to dictate educational content and the values to which their children are exposed? Are there limits on how far we can go in privatizing education without jeopardizing our nation's form of government? If an individual school – public or private – is allowed to determine its curriculum with little oversight, might the state be abdicating its responsibility to protect children and ensure an educated citizenry?

Policy makers need to be aware of the underlying assumptions of various options to privatize education and how each model balances accountability to shareholders, consumers, and the general public. If the purposes and basic structure of public education in our nation are being redefined, we need to understand all implications of the decisions. We need to consider the values that are guiding educational policy into the next century because much more than public schooling is at stake. If we are not attentive, we may, by default, embrace policies that are inconsistent with democratic principles, when a majority of our citizens still believe strongly in these ideals.

References

AMERICAN FEDERATION OF TEACHERS (1994) *The Private Management Of Public Schools: An Analysis Of The EAI Experience In Baltimore* (Washington, DC: AFT.)

Associacion de Puerto Rico Maestros v. Torres, No. 94-371, 1994 WL 780744 (Puerto Rico, 1994).

BENNETT, W. J. (1992) *The De-Valuing Of America: The Fight For Our Culture And Our Children* (New York: Summit Books.)

BUECHLER, M. (1996) *Charter Schools: Legislation and Results After Four Years* (PR-B13) (Bloomington, IN: Indiana Education Policy Center).

Campbell v. Manchester Board of School Directors, 641 A.2d 352 (Vt. 1994).

CARNOY, M. (1995, July 12) Is school privatization the answer? Data from the experience of other countries suggest not. *Education Week*, **40**, 52.

CHUBB, J. E. and MOE, T. M. (1990) *Politics, Markets, And America's Schools* (Washington, DC: Brookings Institute).

DOYLE, D. (1994) The role of private sector management in public education. *Phi Delta Kappan*, **76**, 128–132.

DOYLE, D. (1996) Education supply: will it create demand? *Education Week* (20 March 1996), 48.

Education Daily (1994) NEA puts money behind preserving public education. *Education Daily* (8 July 1994), 1–2.

Education Week (1995) State oversight play a part in success of charter schools. *Education Week* (15 November 1995), 3–4.

Education Daily (1996) EAI eyes short-term deals. *Education Daily* (14 February 1996), 1–2.

FOWLER, F. C. (1991) The shocking ideological integrity of Chubb and Moe. *Journal of Education*, **173**, 119–129.

Gatton v. Goff, Nos 96CVH-01-193, 96CVH-01-721 (Ohio Ct. C.P. 1996).

GLENN, C. (1990) Parent choice in four nations, in W. L. Boyd and H. J. Walberg (eds), *Choice In Education* (Berkeley, CA: McCutchan).

GRAVES, P. (1995) Putting pay on the line. *The School Administrator*, **52**(6), 8–15.

HOFF, D. (1993) State legislators embrace charter schools over choice. *Education Daily* (4 June 1993), 3.

HOUSTON, P. (1994) Making watches or making music. *Phi Delta Kappan*, **76**, 133–135.

MARTINEZ, V., KEMERER, F. and GOODWIN, K. (1993) *Who Chooses And Why* (Denton, TX: University of North Texas).

MARTINEZ, V., THOMAS, K. and KEMERER, F. (1994) Who chooses and why: a look at five school district choice plans. *Phi Delta Kappan*, **75**, 578–681.

McCARTHY, M. (1995) Private investment in public education: boon or boondoggle? *Journal of School Leadership*, **5**, 4–21.

McGRIFF, D. (1995) Lighting the way for systemic reform. *School Administrator*, **57**(7), 14–19.

McLAUGHLIN, J. (1992) Schooling for profit: capitalism's new frontier. *Educational Horizons*, **71**, 23–30.

McLAUGHLIN, J. (1995) Public education and private enterprise. *School Administrator*, **52**(7), 7–12.

OIA (1994) More on private management of schools *OIA Info Memo, Organization Of Institutional Affiliates* (VA: American Educational Research Association), 9–10.

OLSON, L. (1993) Choice for the long haul. *Education Week* (17 November 1993), 27–29.

PIPHO, C. (1995) The expected and the unexpected. *Phi Delta Kappan,* **76**, 742–743.

PONESSA, J. (1995) Cease-fire marks opening of Pennsylvania school in privatization war. *Education Week* (13 September 1995), 6.

PRESIDENT'S COMMISSION ON PRIVATIZATION (1988) *Privatization: Toward More Effective Government* (Washington, DC: US Government Printing Office).

RICHARDSON, J. (1996) Carlson vows aggressive fight for choice plan in Minesota. *Education Week* (24 January 1996), 14.

ROTHSTEIN, R. and RASELL, E. (eds) (1993) *School Choice: Examining The Evidence* (Arlington, VA: Public Interest Publications).

School Administrator (1995) Private firms in the school marketplace (1995) *School Administrator,* **52**(7), 8.

School Board News (1993) Private firm will run Minneapolis schools. (1993) *School Board News* (23 November 1993), 1, 6.

School Board News (1994) EAI overstates student progress in its schools. *School Board News* (21 June 1994), 7.

School Board News (1995) Vouchers help poor children attend private schools. (1995) *School Board News* (5 September 1995), 5.

SEMPLE, M. (1995) Legal issues in charter schooling. *School Administrator,* **52**(7), 24–26.

WALSH, M. (1995a) Baltimore vote ends city's contract with EAI. *Education Week* (6 December 1995), 6.

WALSH, M. (1995b) Sylvan makes quiet inroads into public schools. *Education Week* (29 November 1995), 3, 12.

WALSH, M. (1996a) Brokers pitch education as hot investment. *Education Week* (21 February 1996), 1, 15.

WALSH, M. (1996b) EAI gets contract to develop New York district budget. *Education Week* (21 February 1996), 14.

WALSH, M. (1996c) Hartford ousts EAI in dispute over finances. *Education Week* (31 January 1996), 1, 9.

WINSCHROTT, D. J. and KILGORE, S. B. (1996) *Educational Choice Charitable Trust: An Experiment In School Choice* (Indianapolis: Hudson Institute).

Wisconsin v. Jackson, 546 N.W. 2d 140 (Wis. 1996) *on remand,* No. 95-CV1982 (Wis. Cir. Ct. 1997).

WITTE, J., BAILEY, A. and THORN, C. (1993) *Third-Year Report: Milwaukee Parental Choice Program* (Madison, WI: University of Wisconsin-Madison).

Witters v. Washington Department of Services for the Blind, 474 U.S. 481 (1986).

WOHLSTETTER, P. and ANDERSON, L. (1994) What can US charter schools learn from England's grant-maintained schools? *Phi Delta Kappan,* **75**, 486–491.

Zobrest v. Catalina Foothills School District, 113 S. Ct. 2462 (1993).

9.   *Redefining schooling and community in post-Soviet Kazakstan*

Alan J. DeYoung
University of Kentucky

Bakhytkul Nadirbekyzy
Kazakh State Academy of Management

Children, you must study. And you must study for deep understanding. For those who do, your lives will be enlightened and all your dreams come true. (Ibyrai Altynsarin, mid-nineteenth century Kazak intellectual).

The great rush to rediscover and redefine national secular heroes following the 1991 collapse of the USSR is one part of the story of school reform in Kazakstan today. A new expertise is unfolding in this country as educators are freed from constraints of the Soviet system. Parents have a new opportunity to make national educational policy more responsive to their needs. Unfortunately the economic, political, and social conditions surrounding Kazakstan's schools devastate these potentialities.

Tokash Bokin was a Kazak military leader of the Bolshevik forces during Russia's Civil War. Afterwards, when heroes and place names were chosen by USSR government officials, many schools were named for him in his native Kazakstan. One place named for Tokash Bokin is a rural school in the Zhambul district of Almaty, about 60 miles from the nation's capital. Soviets dubbed the village school 'New Life'. Like most villages in Soviet Central Asia, Akkanar was literally created overnight by Russian, German, Caucasian, and Kazak farming families assigned to work on a collective farm. At that time, the village was named 'Prudky' or 'ponds' by district administrators. By 1994, most of the Russian and German families had left the region for homes either in the city or in the distant lands of their ancestors – leaving primarily rural Kazaks to reclaim the village.

'Prudky' has been changed into 'Akkanar', Kazak for 'source of white water'. Other Kazak heroes from the nineteenth century have likewise been officially resurrected, including Poet Abai Kunabaev, for whom the former national pedagogical university was renamed in 1995, and Zhambul Dzhabaev, namesake of the Akkanar Raion (district) whose 150th birthday was in August 1996.

Tokash Bokin remains the name of the school in Akkanar today because even though he was a Red Army hero, and thus a Soviet figure, he was an ethnic Kazak who gave his live to the Bolshevik cause during the country's civil war (1918–21). And during this era, many Kazaks believed that a Bolshevik government – publicly dedicated to democracy and the rights of workers – had to be an improvement over those of the colonialist Russian Czar. Stalin, of course, proved them wrong.

0268–0939/97 $12 · 00 © 1997 Taylor & Francis Ltd.

The Soviet school model 1920s to 1980s

Pre-1991 colonialist and Soviet education goals are a prerequisite to understanding Kazakstan's educational situation. Formerly, all Russian and then Soviet schools were run directly from Moscow. Lenin's aims for Soviet schools were comparatively progressive. Among European nations, only the fledgling Soviet Union proposed universal schooling for children, citing a citizenry deserving of public investment to ensure full and equal civil participation. An initial burst of educational thinking and innovation in the new Soviet state had a progressive Western flavor echoing the works of John Dewey as well as Russian thinkers (Eklof 1993, Holmes *et al.* 1995, Jones 1994).

Unfortunately, Lenin's programmes disappeared under Stalinist party reforms. By the 1930s, educational policy, like economic and military policy, became highly bureaucratic and dominated by national and economic planning interests, rather than by interests of local communities, teachers, or educational theorists:

> ...the Stalinist school was an integral part of what the ideology of perestroika labelled the 'administrative-command' system...education was characterised by a 'top-down' approach: vertical lines of authority extended downward from the ministries through the regional and district authorities (ronos, goronos) to the directors of schools, teachers, and ultimately pupils. (Eklof 1993: 3)

Consequently, Soviet students typically excelled in mathematics and the hard sciences as a result of technological aims throughout their curriculum (Jones 1994). Yet, Soviet educators were forced to ignore theory and practise pursued in other nations which underscored the importance of individual differences in student abilities, and stages of child development and learning histories (Holmes *et al.* 1995). Official policy uniformly stressed equal rather than different curricular efforts on behalf of children's learning, and during the Stalin years those educators who disagreed were labeled counter-revolutionaries and jailed.

Much Western philosophy and literature was eschewed as elitist individualism, and Western notions about the superiority of philosophical and conceptual knowledge were officially rejected in the USSR in favor of the 'dignity of productive labor'. In Soviet thought, Marx, Engels, and Lenin had discovered the 'truth' of collective life and the organizing role of the Communist Party. The job of educators was to support policies and institutions which would create the new Soviet citizen, and not to question or challenge the emerging orthodoxy of the USSR. Official pronouncements about the dignity and equality of technical and applied labor concealed the fact that by the 1980s most parents with any influence were helping their children avoid vocational schools and using the university as an avenue to upward social mobility (Jones 1994).

Educators were disadvantaged under the former Soviet education system because the structure for educational research and development was centralized. In the USA, such work is partly directed by federal and state agencies, and there are few federally funded centres for research and dissemination, but there are also myriad private foundations, university-funded centres, private think-tanks, and groups affiliated with private corporations and individual school districts, to say nothing of the agendas of thousands of individual researchers and designers of curricular materials. In the USSR, virtually all these activities were planned and conducted by a single Academy of Pedagogical Sciences (APS) through a group of 15 research institutes. Decisions about what directions to pursue, and perhaps more importantly, what directions should not be pursued, were made centrally (Kerr 1993: 477).

The Soviet model of schooling applied in Central Asia

Kazakstan's educational problems, however, even precede those forced by the top-down curricular and administrative approaches of the USSR. Kazakstan is not European, Slavic, Western or Christian. Nineteenth-century Russian colonization and later Soviet incorporation left cultural and imperialist heritages which influence current educational conditions.

In the nineteenth century, Central Asia was to Russia as India was to England and Africa to France. Russians viewed Kazaks as uncivilized nomads under-utilizing vast agricultural areas. In the south and west, Islamic Sultanates of Bukhara, Kokand, and Khiva were the wrong 'civilizing' influences in Moscow's eyes (Rywkin 1990). Prior to Russian colonization, the few formal schools were Islamic training centres taught in Arabic.

By the end of the nineteenth century, all of Central Asia had fallen to advances of the Czarist armies. The territory which became Kazakstan was initially 'civilized' by establishing land reforms which prevented nomadic migration, forced tribal groups to accept Russian governors, encouraged immigration of non-Asian ethnic groups into the Asian Steppe, and replaced the Islamic schools with Russian schools dominating the curriculum with Russian language and civilization. Formal schooling was prvided to only a fraction of the population until the 1930s and the Soviet era.

> Moscow made abundantly clear that its centrally controlled development strategy would favor the needs of the centre above those of the periphery, the requirements of industrialization over those of agriculture, and, of course, the interests of Russians over those of Kazaks. The development strategy chosen – that is, collectivization and nationalization of almost all property in the rural sector – was especially devastating to the Kazaks; traditional Kazakh culture defined a man [sic] through the animals he owned, making private ownership of livestock almost the definition of what it was to be a Kazakh. As might be expected, then, the Kazaks strongly resisted nationalization and when necessary sacrificed their lives and the lives of their animals to try to prevent its introduction. The Kazakh community that survived confiscation was a broken one, its traditional leadership weakened and stripped of many age-old functions; the survivors were malleable and hence of greater value as Soviet citizens. (Olcott 1987: 248).

As was the case throughout the USSR, ideological and scientific training serving industrial development and scientific agriculture eclipsed other educational aims. Social progress meant commitment to Soviet socialism, and offered upward social mobility through the school system primarily via membership in the Communist Party. Rising through the ranks of youth groups in the schools (Octoberists, Young Pioneers, and Komsomol) and obtaining required technical skills were prerequisites of all those who desired occupational success:

> Party membership virtually assured a young Kazhak a sinecure for life. . .The children of shepherds no longer had to share their fathers' fates if they were willing to pay the cost of participation, which was formal subscription to an official ideology that asserted the primacy of Moscow over all the republics and the superiority of the Russian culture over all national ones. . .The Kazakh aspirant who want[ed] to rise in ooblast, republic, or all-union politics [had to] be Russian-speaking and [had to] look and behave as a Russian [did]. He need not be assimilated but he [had to] appear assimilated, so as not to 'stick out' in Russian dominated settings any more than his unusual facial characteristics [made] necessary. The Kazakh candidate [had to] also work harder than his Russian competitor and prove himself more loyal. (Olcott 1987: 248–249)

Perestroika and Glasnost

The unravelling of Soviet education and its ethnic dominance began in the USSR in the mid-1980s with Perestroika and Glasnost. 'Uskorenia' (or acceleration) was the initial phase of Perestroika (restructuring), a general movement begun as an effort to reform the economic system by improving manufacturing efficiency. Another part of this movement was 'Demokratizasia', a process which would theoretically empower factory work brigades to become involved with setting product standards and timetables for more efficient production. Yet, the structural problems of the Soviet economy proved too deep to be solved by top–down administrative mandates and workers' limited control over economic imperatives. This led to the period of 'Glasnost' or openness from 1988, a period of wider social and economic criticism which led to the eventual dismemberment of the Soviet Union and to the creation of many new independent republics, like Kazakstan.

Perestroika, Glasnost, and the hopes of professional educators

During the late 1980s, reformist educators throughout the former Soviet Union became vocal supporters of school improvement notions counter to official peda-gogy. Significant educational changes followed the larger political and economic reforms, and educational reformers championed the rights of children, reducing bureaucracy, and increased parent and communities' involvement.

> [T]he increasing official emphasis upon 'the human factor' privileged education in the rhetoric of perestroika, for if the suc-cess of reform depended, in the long term, upon fostering qualities of initiative, independence and responsibility, what could be more logical than to begin with the schools? Thus, the period 1985–1987 witnessed the emergence of a campaign for greater teacher autonomy in the classroom and for new approaches to the child. (Eklof 1993: 9)

With the waning of Communist Party control of state and national education minis-tries, debates raged in post-Soviet republics about the direction and organization of public schooling. The reformist Russian Education Minister Dneprov championed 10 primary restructuring objectives in the early 1990s. And most other new republics had similar philosophical aims (Dneprov et al. 1993). Five Russian Federation goals targeted school organization: democratization; administrative decentralization; mul-tiplicity; variability; and 'alternativnost' (alternative schooling models). The others focused upon curriculum and instruction: making schools more child centred; differ-entiation of learning based on student interests and abilities; lifelong education; and developmentalism (emphasizing active inquiry). All of these aims were to be under-taken upon the assumption that the school ought to be 'in advance' of society (Eklof 1993). Furthermore, the needs of disenfranchised minority groups throughout the republics was recognized as a major problem:

> [T]he philosophy of standardised, socialised schooling for all Russian youth, with its common curriculum and uniform teaching methods, no longer could meet the needs of an increasingly privatised and decentralised society...Innovative educators identified with individual needs and specific cultural-ethnic group demands of different republics. (Holmes et al. 1995: 276)

Complicating the picture: the experience of Kazakstan

Unfortunately, the costs of the transition to market economies throughout the former USSR have been particularly disastrous for education. Minus a command structure, teachers' salaries, heating bills, and equipment purchases are not met. Some republics became intent on private sector investments rather than social investments, like schools and hospitals. The economic chaos following Soviet collapse led dedicated teachers to quit for lack of pay. Younger and potentially more innovative teachers were the first to leave, bequeathing the old curricula and teaching methods to those who remained (Dneprov *et al.* 1993, Holmes *et al.* 1995).

In addition to economic woes, former central Asian republics like Kazakstan had to recreate (or create) their ethnic and national heritage. The Kazaks were physically and culturally decimated by Russia and the USSR (Olcott 1987). Thus, efforts to repatriate self-exiled Kazaks from China and Mongolia were undertaken in hopes of increasing the percentage of Kazaks living in the territory of Kazakstan. Descriptions of the deeds of great batyrs – ethnic heroes of previous centuries – are found throughout the schools today as are most recent contributions of pre-Soviet statesmen and nationalist parties of the early twentieth century. Pictures of Kazak intellectuals purged and killed by Stalin in the 1930s also dot the walls of many schools throughout the land. The greatest nation-building challenge is rediscovering and teaching the national history of Kazak, a native Turkic language which is not even a usable second language for most urban, professional Kazaks. Fewer than 1% of Kazakstan's ethnic Russians (who comprise less than 40% of the nation's population) speak Kazak. They have appealed in an effort to restore Russian as at least an equal language under the new national constitution. Kazak instruction is complicated further by lack of textbooks and difficulty in obtaining trained teachers. Recruiting teachers and developing texts are viewed by the Ministry of Education as its most serious contemporary problems (Jurinov 1996).

Despite such challenges, Kazakstan is comparatively advantaged in terms of human capital. Most of the population is literate, and mathematical and technical skills are well dispersed throughout the population. The national literacy rate is over 90%, and almost 3.8 million school-aged children were officially enrolled during the 1993–94 academic year. So too, women's status is arguably better in terms of education, occupational participation, and civil rights than in many other Muslim countries. As in most developed nations, many highly educated women were among the ranks of teachers – once a highly valued status in Kazakstan and throughout the former USSR.

A cautionary note is exerted over reconstructing a usable past for ethnic Kazaks because there are over 100 different ethnic groups in Kazakstan today. Each is worried about status in the new republic, now clearly dominated by ethnic Kazaks. Some of the larger minority ethnic groups have instruction in their native languages; but will minority ethnic interests be any better represented in Kazak schools in the future than they were in former Soviet schools?

Another cultural caution is raised in considering how much evil can be attributed to the Russian and Soviet colonizers of the past hundred years when vestiges are still powerfully present. Many Russian ethnics who have known only Kazakstan as home for three or four generations believe that Kazakstan is still part of Russia. A resurgence of Russian nationalism in the late 1990s and the fact that Russian ethnics populate many northern Kazak Oblasts prompt fears that Russia may try to reintegrate half of Kazakstan. Meanwhile, Russia remains the largest trading partner of Kazakstan. Kazakstan places its greatest immediate economic hopes on its huge oil reserves, yet transportation of oil must go through Caspian Sea ports controlled by Moscow.

On responsiveness and expertise

Recent economic circumstances and political decisions in Kazakstan have a mixed effect on the nation's education system. Since independence, government revenues have been in decline and corruption has been widespread.

> Although the government's intentions may have been good, and although a number of people have made money since independence, including some who have acquired large private fortunes, in general Kazakstan's economy has traced a vertiginous decline since independence...The impact of this decline on the population has been pronounced. In 1993, inflation was approximately 2,500%...Wage increases have not kept pace with inflation: real wages declined by 33% across the republic during the first half of 1994, with greater losses in northern Kazakstan, where workers on average lost more than half their spending power. Inflation compounds the impact of industrial unemployment, which has begun to spread through the economy in both open forms and more-disguised ones, such as reduced workweeks, forced vacations, and long periods in which workers are not paid. (Olcott 1995: 282–283).

Kazakstan's freedom allowed new models of schooling in response to economic conditions. Parents have choices of schools and curricula which are still controlled by the Kazak Ministry of Education (MoE). Now there are over two dozen officially sanctioned curricular types, mostly diverging at the secondary level. Some schools emphasize humanities instruction (the Gymnasium); so retain heavy emphasis on Mathematics and Sciences (the Lycea). Some curricula are taught primarily in Kazak, others primarily in Russian. Some schools are 'magnet' secondary schools which specialize in foreign language instruction (English, for instance) or business and economics courses preparatory to higher education institutes specializing in similar undertakings. Links between higher education institutions and secondary schools are formal. Contemporary Kazak education promotes schools that respond to differences in children's interests and certainly to parents' interests at secondary levels.

On the other hand, approximately 30% of the nation's teachers left their jobs in 1993 for work in the private sector as government support for public schools fell from over 8% of the nation's budget to 3.6% in 1995 (Jurinov 1996). In 1995, the MoE projected 22,323 teacher vacancies in the country. The monthly salary of a teacher with a normal teaching load in 1995 was 2700 Tenge, or about US$ 41. Yet, teachers are rarely paid on time, and salaries are delivered two to three months late. Few teachers try to live on one teacher's salary, with the government admitting that 2700 Tenge was the average monthly food cost. In 1996, the MoE also pronounced that only 57% of the costs of schooling in the country is paid for by government sources and that only about 20% of students in the country could afford to buy textbooks no longer to be supplied free.

The fiscal crisis in schooling in Kazakstan suggests that although post-Soviet educators there today enjoy much greater freedom in developing innovative programmes, socioeconomic forces intervene in this 'expertise'. More affluent parents partly or primarily subsidize what were once public schools. Better teachers and better facilities are found in those secondary schools where parents can afford to pay the equivalent of $20 or $30 extra per month for their children's education. These schools can afford to hire the best teachers, to heat their buildings, and to purchase computers and software. Unfortunately, most parents in Kazakstan do not have extra money to spend on education, even though formal education remains highly valued. Furthermore, it is the announced intention of the government to divest itself of most public pre-school programmes and vocational programmes, transferring such to a pay-for-services basis. Higher education, too, is the target of reform, and the Ministry of Education seeks to decrease by 25–30% the number of government-supported students, replacing them with fee-paying students.

In 1996 the President and Education Minister publicly proclaimed that private schools would increase the quality of education in the nation and expand parental choices. Neither addressed the implications for unequal social and occupational futures for poorer children and children of different ethnic groups.

Return to Tokash Bokin

At Tokash Bokin, enrollments are less than half school capacity with 458 students. When the school was first freed from Soviet control, a new computer lab was installed and hands-on Western style economics training curriculum was constructed. Today, however, there is no computer teacher and no money for the economics programme. Furthermore, several classes are taught by retired teachers as no other teachers are available.

The Kazak rural schools face similar teacher shortage problems to US rural schools. The school curriculum varies daily, which enables city teachers to move from school to school as their schedules permit.

Being hours away from the city, Tokash Bokin cannot rely on moonlighting teachers, but over half of the school's 45 teachers teach more than the usual number of hours. In addition, Tokash Bokin teachers are paid three or four months late, thus having to depend upon their extended family resources to survive. Such financial conditions contribute to teachers leaving or changing jobs. The second author of this paper made this choice herself. The fact that teaching conditions are also very difficult compounds the problem. In the three days of our February school interviews, there was no heat or electricity in school. The room temperature never rose above freezing. All teaching supplies were bought by teachers and parents rather than the MoE.

Parents of Tokash Bokin are highly responsive now that Moscow no longer controls education. Their activism is due partly to national ethnic foment. Parents throughout the former USSR are replacing the socialization once provided by the Communist Party and its youth groups. Today there is a very active Parent Committee at Tokash Bokin which works with teachers on citizenship and academic problems of students. This group has raised funds for building repair projects and supplies similar to activists in many US schools.

Parents also have helped Tokash Bokin respond to new schooling opportunities in the nation via Kazak culture. Tokash Bokin is organized into a formal morning curriculum (9 a.m. to 2 p.m.), followed by an active after-school programme. The afternoon programme includes several subjects long established in the Soviet labor-oriented curriculum, like agriculture and industrial arts. Peoples' Pedagogics, introduced in the late 1980s, focuses on nineteenth-century nomadic Kazak traditions, art, symbols, music, weaving, legends, etc. Since Peoples' Pedagogics predates the new formal focus on Kazakstan's history in the morning curriculum, parents and grandparents aid younger teachers in such subjects.

We conclude that public education in Kazakstan and perhaps throughout the former Soviet Union faces a variety of unexpected problems and issues. Education, of course, is about values. Educational leaders in the USSR just before the break-up argued that the school could lead the culture, beliefs with which modern educators would likely concur. Equality of educational opportunity is a powerful antecedent to a private sector which operates upon the norm of inequality. In the rush to a market economy, confronted by a scarcity of educational resources, Kazakstan is moving away from the educational equity which was once perhaps the most admirable voiced objective of the former Soviet Union. Expertise is becoming increasingly available in Kazakstan to those children whose parents can afford to pay extra for better teachers and better facilities. For rural and impoverished schools, the future remains bleak. In Kazakstan, tensions between expertise and responsiveness are the conundrum of its schools' past and future.

References

DNEPROV, E. D., LAZEREV, V. S. and SOBKIN, V. S. (1993) The state of education in Russia today, in B. Eklof and E. Dneprov (eds), *Democracy And The Russian School: The Reform Movement In Education Since 1984* (Boulder, CO: Westview Press).

EKLOV, B. (1993) Democracy in the Russian school: educational reform since 1984, in B. Eklof and E. Dneprov (eds), *Democracy And The Russian School: The Reform Movement In Education Since 1984* (Boulder, CO: Westview Press).

HOLMES, B., READ, G. and VOSKRESENSKAYA, N. (1995) *Russian Education: Tradition and Transition* (New York: Garland).

JONES, A. (1994) The soviet legacy, in A. Jones (ed.), *Educational And Society In The New Russia* (Armonk, NY: M.E. Sharpe), 3–23).

JURINOV, M. (1996) *About The Present Condition And Development Perspectives Of The Higher Education System Of The Republic Of Kazakstan* (Almaty, KZ: Report to the Cabinet of Ministers).

KERR, S. (1993) USSR, in P. Cookson, A. Sednovik and S. Semel (eds), *International Handbook of Educational Reform* (New York: Greenwood Press), 473–493.

OLCOTT, M. B. (1987) *The Kazaks* (Stanford, CA: Hoover Institution Press).

OLCOTT, M. B. (1995) *The Kazaks*, 2nd edn (Stanford, CA: Hoover Institution Press).

RYWKIN, M. (1990) *Moscow's Muslim Challenge: Soviet Central Asia* (London: M.E. Sharpe).

10.   Parents and children: representations of family understanding parents' and teachers' internal working models of their roles in children's lives

Sandra T. Azar
Frances L. Hiatt School of Psychology
Clark University, Worcester, MA

The focus of my work has primarily been on the origins of violence in close relationships, particularly in parent–child relationships, not on how schools and families relate to one another. The framework in which this work has been done, however, has, I believe, tremendous relevance for understanding the origins of negative transactions between parents and teachers. This framework emphasizes the role of expectations, interpretations, and attributions of causality in producing conflict in interpersonal relationships (Azar 1986, 1989). These internal processes may play a similar role in determining the quality of transactions between schools and families. In this chapter, it will be argued that teachers may make interpretations regarding the meaning of parental behaviour that are based in a different social reality than that in which many families live. Parents, in turn, may come to their transactions with schools with a set of assumptions based in their own negative academic experiences and in erroneous or negatively biased beliefs about schools and teachers. Both situations can lead to conflict.

Essentially, the thesis of this chapter is that parents and teachers may have different internal working models of each other's 'work'. Because of this fact, their transactions at times are marked by an adversarial tone rather than a collaborative one. In the process, children's loyalties are tested and their best interests are not served. While this discrepancy in models has probably always existed, I will argue that with recent structural, economic, and cultural changes in today's families, the gap has increased sharply.

The social cognitive theorizing regarding relationships in which I and others have been engaged emphasizes the importance of identifying differences in people's working assumptions about relationships before collaborative efforts can occur (Azar 1989). I will briefly describe this theory and research on family conflict. These will then be used to discuss how teachers' and parents' transactions may similarly result in conflict, as well as ways they might 're-think' their interpretive approach to each other.

Social cognitive theory

Social cognitive theorists believe that as we go through the world, we have little road maps in our heads about how the world works and how people 'should' relate to

0268–0939/97 $12 · 00 © 1997 Taylor & Francis Ltd.

one another (Heider 1958, Bandura 1986). These maps or knowledge structures include the defining qualities of important social roles in society, as well as how individuals in these roles should behave. These guides make our transactions with others and the world less arduous and more 'automatized' (Fiske and Taylor 1991). That is, we can respond to others without thinking too hard about the meaning of their behaviour and the nature of our responses.

Social cognitive theorists call these road maps schemata. We have a schema for 'living rooms' for example. When you hear the word 'living room', most of us conjure up an image of a room with a couch, a chair, a coffee table perhaps, and maybe a few lamps. In the midst of this picture, however, the presence of a cow would be jarring. Cows in our culture do not 'belong' in a living room. If one were to be there, we would be looking around for a cause. That is, our expectations about how things 'should be' guide our reactions (e.g. trigger our search for causal explanations and our affective response to the events we encounter). In my example, we look for someone to blame for this 'abnormal' state of affairs and might experience confusion or frustration.

The concept of a 'script' extends this idea one step further by positing that we have internal models of a domain of responses (action sequences) that are appropriate within various social settings or within certain roles. At professional conferences, we have internalized a set of actions that can be expected. Presenters give talks, show slides, and attend cocktail parties. A presenter dancing on the table would be incongruent with our 'conference' schema and 'presenter at a symposium' script. We might have a moment of dismay (and perhaps humor), but ultimately we might apply a label to this person of 'unprofessional', 'eccentric', or 'troubled'. Ultimately, if we were asked to consider this person's work again for a conference, we might think of our label of 'unprofessional' and this might lead us to reject his or her paper as probably not being of much value. That is, once a model of an individual is formed, we may selectively attend to those facts which reinforce this model (Fiske and Taylor 1991), thus maintaining it even if it is biased. This is most likely to happen if we have rigid expectations regarding 'appropriate' conference behaviour. If our schemata are more flexible, however, we might more carefully consider the content of the submission and then make a decision.

Schemata, scripts, and conflict in relationships

Because these 'road maps' or schemata regarding the world and relationships grow out of a combination of our unique individual experiences and the cultures or subcultures in which we live (i.e. prevailing cultural beliefs; Goodnow 1988), there are individual differences in their content. That is, the schemata and scripts people have regarding social roles like parent or child or teacher may vary. This means that the same event can have widely varying meanings. Take one incident as an example. You are waiting in line at a movie theatre. Someone pushes you. You could interpret the push as an accident and dismiss it by saying to yourself, 'This is a very close space. It is hard for this not to happen.' The content of this 'self talk' is founded in a basic schema that people do not go out of their way to hurt others.

In contrast, you could have a much more malevolent interpretation: 'This guy is trying to cut in line' or 'He intentionally is trying to push me.' In this case, you may react more negatively, become angry, feel frustrated and, perhaps, a fight might ensue. Here, a relationship script may be operating that includes the assumption that people often try to hurt others (a negative relationship schema). Even if you engage in this second type of interpretive process, you may still have good problem-solving skills and generate other more neutral explanations for this person's behaviour (e.g. 'he's probably having a bad day'). This would act to calm you down (e.g. 'It's not worth making a big deal about this') and you are less likely to experience and engage openly in conflict. Without such problem-solving skills, conflict is more likely.

Social cognition and child abuse

Nowhere may interpretive processes be more important than in parenting. The motivation of young children's behaviour, especially before they have language, must be interpreted. Young children are less able to communicate their needs, thoughts, and feelings, leaving room for a variety of parental interpretations (Azar 1989). Parents selectively marking and responding to children's actions are believed to be crucial in guiding children toward more sophisticated means of responding (Rogoff *et al.* 1984). Parents must develop a fine-tuned ability to identify acts in their offspring as meaningful and worthy of response. Parents' beliefs or schemata regarding children's ability and how children and parents should relate serve as filters through which child-rearing situations are viewed, interpretations made, and responses chosen. The attributions made to one's offspring's behaviour, unlike those made with adults, need to take into consideration their developmental level. That is, parents must be exquisitely sensitive to the child's perspective in order to interpret behaviour and respond appropriately (Miller 1988), facilitating children's continued growth.

Developmentally appropriate schemata also help parents deal with the stress of childrearing (e.g. facilitate smooth parent–child transactions). That is, parents can always attribute their children's non–compliance or aversive behaviour to the task or to their immaturity (e.g. 'She's only two. She doesn't understand. I need to explain it better'). Because of a positive bias toward children, they can even construct a positive explanation (e.g. 'Isn't she strong willed') and not attribute it either to their own parenting inadequacy or their children's intentional misbehaviour. They can also search for external causes ('There was too much going on and he was distracted'). Based on cognitive models of stress management and aggression (Ferguson and Rule 1983), such interpretations would reduce the parents' negative affective response and allow them to respond in a calmer and more thoughtful manner.

If parents' beliefs or expectations are overly rigid, inappropriate or inaccurate, however, then the interpretations made of children's behaviour will also be inappropriate and, ultimately, lead them to maladaptive and inadequate parenting responses. This model posits that there is a great variation in parents' schemata regarding 'children'.

Our research has shown that child-abusive parents possess unrealistically high and rigid expectations regarding children's roles, especially in relation to parents (i.e. they see them as 'little adults'; Larrance and Twentyman 1983, Azar 1986, 1988, 1989, Barnes and Azar 1990). When they encounter situations where they are unable to get their children to do a difficult task, their disturbed scripts do not allow them to ascribe failure to external factors or to developmental factors which would reduce the impact of this stressor. Consequently, they attribute inappropriate levels of blame to themselves (e.g. 'If I was a better parent, I could get him to do this') or to their child (i.e. labeling of their child in negative dispositional or intent terms: 'He's just a brat'; 'He's out to get me'). The former attribution cannot be held for too long. Indeed, a self-protective bias has been demonstrated to exist in the attributions individuals make for failure (Miller and Ross 1975). When we fail, we are more likely to attribute it to something external.

Parents who continually encounter 'failures' with their children, therefore, will begin to identify the locus of responsibility within the child and then proceed to over-react and label the child as 'being evil', 'bad', or intentionally trying to get to them. This may be particularly likely when the parent is under great stress. Over time and many encounters, a negative bias toward the child may develop (e.g. 'He's hopeless.' 'He's no good.' 'She doesn't care.').

Such attributions lead to greater use of punishment and less calm and helpful communications (e.g. use of explanation in discipline situations; Barnes and Azar 1990). Parents would take less pleasure in the success experiences they have with their children, find the failures more aversive and, overall, feel less competent. Indeed, they may also be less likely to see themselves as a socialization agent with their children (e.g. they are less likely to give teaching as a reason for their engaging in discipline). So, conflict in parent–child relationships may have its roots in inappropriate schemata regarding children and the negative meaning assigned to children's behaviour.

Social cognitive theory and the relationship between schools and families

So what relevance does this model have for relationships between families and schools? Before I elaborate on this, I will briefly describe a series of incidents that I believe will give you a flavor of the link. These examples hint at inappropriate expectations, faulty assumptions, and misinterpretations that might exist when teachers and parents transact with each other. These incidents focus on places where teachers may mislabel parental behaviour. Parents too may have erroneous beliefs regarding schools and teachers and these will be discussed later.

The first incident happened in an undergraduate seminar I teach. I typically begin the family course by asking students to discuss any 'special' experiences they have with 'families'. In this particular class, there were two students who had just completed their student teaching. Both had more than one experience – one in a suburban school and the other in an urban, inner-city one. The first student talked about the 'differences' in her experiences with families within these two settings. She noted that the suburban parents were 'so involved...they really cared about their kids', with the implication that the inner-city parents did not. I did not say anything. The second student, taking my silence as a green light to elaborate on this theme, echoed the first's comments. Both students gave as evidence for the parents' 'not caring' the lack of parental presence in the school (e.g. volunteering in the library). They also cited the children sharing some of the little 'horrors' of urban living (e.g. apartment buildings where domestic violence occurred) and a poverty home life (e.g. being put in charge of siblings). Nodding in agreement with each other, these two young women described their view of these parents as deficient in fulfilling their role of parent (e.g. 'They let their children live like this') and inferred they were 'bad' parents.

As I listened, I thought of my clinical work in the homes of inner-city AFDC mothers, a view from the other side of these transactions. I remembered one mother who kept her child home from school. Her child's teacher had asked her daughter to submit her report in a special binder that the family could not afford. She did not want her child embarrassed (or herself for that matter) and so she kept her home. She thought it was the 'only' thing she could do as a parent.

I also thought of a second mother with whom I'd worked in parent counselling who came into my office very unhappy and crying after a school team meeting regarding her child's behavioural problems. Much to my surprise her upset was not about her child's difficulties. It turned out that her son's school was the same one she had attended as a child. This mother had quit school and when she walked through the doors of that school, she was reminded of the sense of failure and rejection that she had felt there many years ago. In tears, she focused on the family background sheet of the team report she was given. They had typed neatly under mother's education 'did not complete high school'. Feeling so incompetent, she had little room left to discuss her child. My guess was that, given her presentation with me, she had probably been labelled 'resistant' or 'non-responsive' to the school personnel, which was confirmed when she referred to the team 'ganging up' on her.

Finally, I thought of a teacher workshop I had on how to talk to parents. A teacher raised his hand and asked me how I would go about convincing a mother that her son was a 'liar'. I was struck with his strong assumption that the mother in question *should* accept this view of her child. He saw it as crucial that she do so if her seven-year-old son was to change.

Each of these incidents might be dismissed as being isolated ones. I, however, believe they are more common than one might think. They reflect common problems in the transactions between schools and families that are based in discrepancies in their social worlds, their schemata regarding each other's role in children's lives, and the scripts they each have for how they should relate to each other. These examples highlight places where teachers might mislabel, misinterpret, or misattribute parents' behaviour in negative ways. I could have just as easily cited examples where parents might do likewise. Certainly, one of the examples hints at this (e.g. the mother describing the teachers as 'ganging up' on her). Such examples highlight potential obstacles to parents and teachers working as collaborative partners in the care of children. They come to the relationship with differing assumptions regarding the meaning of words (e.g. 'involvement', 'being a good parent') and of actions. Assumptions that may interfere with smooth transactions which are crucial for children's well-being.

Given the nature of today's family, more and more community institutions, whether they want to or not, are pushed into being partners in the business of families. If this partnership is to go smoothly – to foster good communiation, mutual respect and a coordinated effort on children's behalf – a reciprocal understanding of the two participants' social reality must occur. Otherwise, similar to child-abusing families, conflict and 'violence' will occur with children as victims.

Nested in my examples are just a few of the faulty assumptions that may cause conflict between parents and teachers. First, there is an assumption that families' 'involvement' in children's lives is something that can be 'seen' or that it will be 'seen' in the school setting. Parent involvement occurs in multiple domains that include meeting emotional needs as well as academic ones. Parents must often select among these needs in making priorities (e.g. a mother choosing to spare her child embarrassment over missing a day at school). This prioritizing may use a different yardstick from that used by teachers.

Second, there are faulty assumptions regarding the realities of today's family (e.g. level of affluence, literacy, etc.). A binder that costs a few dollars may be more than a family can afford. One is forced to be sensitive to the economic realities of parents' lives if we are to be 'successful' in working with such parents. Such concern is needed not only for families on welfare. Today, we have dual-parent working families who fall below the poverty line. Single parents who have multiple demands placed on them may find it difficult to do the 'extras' required by schools (e.g. they may work different shifts to keep child care costs down and may be unable to volunteer at school).

Issues regarding parents' own ability level also cannot be ignored. Notes sent home are often an important means of communicating with parents. Yet, some parents are unable to read. Failure to respond, therefore, may not be evidence of unwillingness to do so. Parents privately share with me that they are unable to help their children with homework because they themselves do not understand how to do it. Yet, teachers may interpret this as evidence of their 'not caring' for them. Indeed, one child quoted his teacher's pressure on him to 'get' his mother to help and implied that there was something wrong with him that his parent had not. The view that parents are not being responsible is reflected even at the federal level. A recent request for proposals from the federal government for projects to increase parental involvement in schools listed as an example: 'projects designed to educate parents regarding their educational responsibilities'. Starting a programme with an assumption of 'irresponsibility' on the parents' part is not likely to foster a partnership with them.

A third 'script' probem evidenced in one of the examples concerns assumptions made by teachers about parents during parent–teacher conferences. These assumptions are that parents feel powerful and that the school can establish an 'encapsulated' relationship with them focused entirely around their child's academic performance. By encapsulated, I mean that it includes them as 'parents', but not as 'former students' or the myriad of other roles they may have (i.e. an essentially compartmentalized 'self'). Gaining an understanding of the parents' own experiences in school may be an important first step in beginning to engage them in a collaborative partnership. In working with abusive parents, we have found it helpful to begin with a discussion of their own experience of discipline growing up (Azar 1989) before trying to work with them about adopting more adaptive discipline strategies.

Finally, illustrated in one of the examples are assumptions that all parents hold as strongly the belief that an education is 'important', and that the teacher is an 'expert' on their children and that if there is a discrepancy in their views, it is 'helpful' for them to adopt a teacher's view of their children for positive change to occur. Clinicians who specialize in parenting work have long recognized that the most unproductive thing one can do in trying to help parents make changes is to tell them that you are expert on matters concerning their children or their role. They have lived with their children for many years and will have to deal with them long after they leave the teacher's classroom. This fact needs to be acknowledged. Indeed, in beginning parent therapy, this is explicitly stated. Parents will often ask the change agent 'Do you have children?' This is often a cue that the parent is getting the idea that the change agent thinks they have more knowledge about their child than they as parent do. Such a stance does not facilitate collaboration.

To summarize, teachers have schemata regarding parents and families just like they have a schema for 'living rooms'. The 'involved' parent schemata, for example, includes working in the school library, helping children with their homework, etc. This schemata, however, may not match those of parents. That is, not all parents view 'involvement' in this way. Chavkin and Williams (1989) for example, found that low-income parents did not differ from middle-income parents in their desire for involvement with their children's education, but that they defined components of involvement differently (i.e. how to be involved) and saw themselves as more pressed for time in having such involvement occur. This fact may lead schools to see some of the families with whom they work as similar to the picture presented earlier of a cow in a living room. Parents' responses violate expectations regarding families. Teachers then search around looking for someone to blame and it is easy to blame parents and then feel comfortable with labeling them as the problem. Indeed, the parents with whom they may have the most trouble may have the most discrepant views of their role.

Sometimes this labeling may act to triangulate children, precipitating a loyalty crisis. For example, saying to the children of uneducated parents that 'not having an education means the world will pass you by' is asking them to accept a view of their parents as somehow damaged or imperfect. Such triangulation may be more likely to occur with socioeconomically disadvantaged parents and culturally different ones. For culturally diverse families, the school system may be just one more institutional setting that is trying to 'rip' the family's history out of their child's psyche. In some cases, a piece of data like a child being kept home from school is taken as evidence of parental irresponsibility, and a negative meaning is attached to it. Teachers may also accept a child's negative representation of his or her parents as the reality (e.g. 'My mom wouldn't help me') and form a coalition with them against the persons who have the greatest potential to impact positively on their lives in the long run. (This same kind of 'splitting' is seen in divorced families and is detrimental to children's development).

Finally, parents may not be treated with respect as people. Parents have histories in the educational system that may interfere with their willingness to engage with it, or they may be fragile about their competence as parents. These factors increase the potential to do them, and ultimately their children, 'violence'. A survey was recently conducted in southern Maine which asked community institutions to cite what they saw as the needs and problems of families today (Hornby et al. 1990). When day care centre staff were surveyed, their responses were 'personal' factors pressing on parents, such as 'parents' lack of time for children and themselves'; 'financial problems'; 'working parent stresses'; 'guilt'; and 'lack of parenting skills'. They chose language that places the locus of causality for problems outside the parents' control. Such language and the positively toned schema regarding parents it may reflect, would allow such professionals to engage in helping responses. Indeed, in my studies of mothers' social supports, those with young children often cite their children's day care as a source of support. This testifies to the level of partnership felt.

In contrast, when the data from schools in the Maine survey are examined, a different picture of 'parents' problems' was portrayed. The top responses regarding the problems faced by families were 'parental substance abuse'; 'dysfunctional family systems'; 'child abuse and neglect'; 'teen pregnancy'; 'homelessness'; and 'single parents'. The more personal language used by the day care staff was much less evident. Causality was intrinsic to parents as people (i.e. very similar to how abusive parents label their children as 'bad' on a dispositional level). This labeling would lead to a distancing of teachers from parents and to teachers being less likely to engage in helping behaviours. Indeed, teachers of young children are more likely than middle-school teachers to engage in parent-involvement strategies (Epstein and Dauber 1991).

When any two professional groups interact there is great potential for epistemological conflict and boundary problems (i.e. what has been called 'jurisdictional disputes' in the sociological literature) (Azar 1992, Moore 1970). The role of parent and the role of teacher in places overlaps. In the day care setting, these roles overlap to a greater extent (e.g. both may diaper children, wipe their noses, etc.) and this perhaps allows the day care staff to identify more with the parent – to see the world as they do. Teachers in high school frequently deal with only parts of parents' roles and, overall, they have less contact with parents. They are responsible for subjects (e.g. math), not children. In addition, in day care settings the issue of consumer is also much clearer [i.e. parents pay for day care directly, not through some anonymous process (e.g. taxes]. The latter may lead to further distancing of the two partners in children's lives. Like strangers waiting in line, if one jostles the other, potential for negative intepretations can occur and can lead to conflict and a triangulation of children.

So far, I have focused on teachers and schools as making inappropriate assumptions or interpretations regarding parents. Parents, too, have unrealistic expectations about teachers that can cause them to be 'abusive' in their transactions with teachers. Table 1 lists some possible ones. Space constraints do not allow as full an elaboration of the distorted interpretations by parents that can occur regarding school and teachers. The fact that parents' internal working models play a role in determining the adversarial nature of contacts as well cannot be ignored.

In summary, it might be argued based on the above discussion that some 're-thinking' of assumptions is required for schools as they transact with parents. In table 2, I have listed some possible working assumptions that work in other contexts to facilitate communication and increase potential for change (e.g. therapy). A similar list might be provided to parents in helping orient them to working more effectively with teachers. Educational programmes that assume a singularity of beliefs or values will be doomed to failure whether they are imposed by legislatures, parents, or schools. When we are trying to change schools or families' relationshps with schools, we are in the realm of relationships. People hold their beliefs about relationships as dearly as they hold religious beliefs. Unless the nature of our respective gods is defined, no coordinated action can take place. As with abusive parents, everyone's 'self' is 'on the line' and the potential 'loss of control' that may come with change is scary for participants. Bateson (1979), a well-known systems theorist, suggested that

Table 1.   Parents' erroneous beliefs about teachers and schools.

1.   Teachers can handle anything (if they want to)
2.   Schools will make up for anything that the parent missed
3.   Schools have the resources to give their child one-on-one attention
4.   Schools have the capability to make every child equally 'well educated'
5.   When things go wrong, teachers want to blame them
6.   If their child is not succeeding, it is their fault
7.   If their child is not succeeding, it is the teacher's fault

Table 2.   Helpful assumptions in working with parents – the basics.

1. Parents do the best they can
2. Parents need to feel a sense of mastery in their role
3. Parents have difficulty being easy on themselves
4. Seeking help with parenting is seen as dangerous
5. Parents are ambivalent about wanting help
6. Parents expect you to tell them they're doing a bad job
7. There is no one right way to parent
8. Change is dangerous
9. Change is slow

creating or re-creating order in any system requires energy. Conflicts that are based in ascribing negative meaning drain energy from systems. An awareness alone of such discrepancy of beliefs can go a long way toward increasing available energy for change. Relationshps need to be based in mutually positive schemata or the development of them. In an article by Goffin (1989), entitled 'How well do we respect the children in our care?', the author suggests a list of ways to show respect. I would like to steal her words and change them to reflect respect for parents and for teachers: (1) show respect for their roles and the difficulties inherent in them; (2) respond with sensitivity to individual differences; (3) develop nurturing relationshps with them; (4) use authority with wisdom to facilitate growth; (5) consider how practises influence them; (6) view mistakes as potential learning opportunities, (7) acknowledge their competencies; (8) acknowledge the expertise needed to carry out their role; and (9) speak out on behalf of parenting and teaching as professions. These suggestions may be helpful, but will require careful understanding of the other's roles to be carried out effectively.

References

AZAR, S. T. (1986) A framework for understanding child maltreatment: an integration of cognitive behavioural and developmental perspectives. *Canadian Journal of Behavioural Science*, **18**, 340–355.

AZAR, S. T. (1988) Childrearing stress and attributional processes: an examination of a cognitive behavioral model of child maltreatment. Paper presented at the annual meeting of the Association for the Advancement of Behavior Therapy, Washington.

AZAR, S. T. (1989) Training parents of abused children, in C. E. Schaefer and J. M. Briesmeister (eds), *Handbook Of Parent Training: Parents As Co-Therapists For Children's Behavior Problems* (New York: Wiley), 414–441.

AZAR, S. T. (1992) Legal issues in the assessment of family violence involving children, in M. Hersen and R. Ammerman (eds), *Handbook Of Assessment In Family Violence* (New York: Guilford), 47–70.

AZAR, S. T., ROBINSON, D., HEKIMIAN, E. and TWENTYMAN, C. T. (1984) Unrealistic expectations and problem solving ability in maltreating and comparison mothers. *Journal of Consulting and Clinical Psychology,* **52**, 687–691.

AZAR, S. T. and ROHRBECK, C. A. (1986) Child abuse and unrealistic expectations: further validation of the parent opinion questionnaire. *Journal of Consulting and Clinical Psychology,* **54**, 867–868.

BANDURA, A. (1986) *Social Foundations Of Thought And Action* (Englewood Cliffs, NJ: Prentice-Hall).

BARNES, K. T. and AZAR, S. T. (1990) Maternal expectations and attributions in discipline situations: a test of a cognitive model of parenting. Paper presented at the annual meeting of the American Psychological Association, Boston, MA.

BATESON, G. (1979) *Mind And Nature* (New York: Bantam Books).

CHAVKIN, N. F. and WILLIAMS, D. L. (1989) Low income parents' attitudes toward parent involvement in education. *Journal of Sociology and Social Welfare*, **16**, 17–28.

EPSTEIN, J. L. and DAUBER, S. L. (1991) School programs and teacher practises of parent involvement in inner-city elementary and middle schools. *The Elementary School Journal*, **91**, 289–305.

FERGUSON, T. J. and RULE, B. G. (1983) An attributional perspective on anger and aggression, in R. Green and E. Donnerstein (eds), *Aggression, Theoretical And Empirical Review*, Vol. I (New York: Academic Press), 41–74.

FISKE, S. T. and TAYLOR, S. E. (1991) *Social Cognition* (New York: McGraw-Hill).

GOFFIN, S. G. (1989) How well do we respect the children in our care? *Childcare Education*, **66**(2), 68–74.

GOODNOW, J. J. (1988) Parent's ideas, actions, and feelings: models and methods from developmental and social psychology. *Child Development*, **59**, 286–320.

HEIDER, F. (1958) *The Psychology Of Interpersonal Relations* (New York: Wiley).

HORNBY, H., HOLLANDER, L. and SCUCCI, T. (1990) *Child Abuse Prevention: A Community Based Approach. Community Assessment Of Child Care Abuse Prevention*, Summary Report, Part I (Portland, ME: National Child Welfare Resource Center for Management and Administration).

LARRANCE, D. T and TWENTYMAN, C. T. (1983) Maternal attributions and child abuse. *Journal of Abnormal Psychology*, **92**, 449–457.

MILLER, D. T and ROSS, M. (1975) Self serving bias in the attribution of causality: fact or fiction› *Psychological Bulletin*, **82**, 213–225.

MILLER, S. (1988) Parent's beliefs about children's cognitive development. *Child Development*, **59**, 259–285.

MOORE, W. E. (1970) *The Profession: Roles And Rules* (New York: Russell Sage).

NELSON, K. (1983) The derivation of concepts and categories from event representatives, in E. K. Skolnick (ed.), *New Trends In Conceptual Representation: Challenges to Piaget's Theory?* (Hillsdale, NJ: Erlbaum).

PLOTKIN, R. (1983) Cognitive mediation in disciplinary actions among mothers who have abused or neglected their children: dispositional and environmental factors. Unpublished doctoral dissertation, University of Rochester.

ROGOFF, B., MALKIN, G. and McBRIDE, K. (1984) Interaction with babies as guidance in development. In B. Rogoff and J. W. Wertsch (eds), *Children's Learning in the 'Zone of Proximal Development'* (San Francisco: Jossey-Bass), pp. 31–44.

SCHANKE, R. C and ABELSON, R. P. (1977) *Scripts, Plans, Goals, And Understanding* (Hillsdale, NJ: Erlbaum).

SHIFFRON, R. M. and SCHNEIDER, W. (1977) Controlled and automatic human information processing, II: Perceptual learning, automatic attending, and a general theory. *Psychological Review*, **84**, 127–190.

11.   *The emerging politics of assessment alternatives: professional revolution versus public values*

Jean Treiman
California Lutheran University

Mahna Schwager
WestEd

During the last two decades school professionals throughout the USA have participated in hundreds of 'bully' reform efforts. Many efforts, such as Clinton's *Goals 2000 Program*, are viewed by professional experts as external or lay efforts at school reform. Professionals often downplay the value and legitimacy of these reforms and see public attempts at school reform as naive, unrealistic, or inspired by the base moral instincts of political self-interest. Emerging from a complex mixture of school reform platforms, the energetic arguments over authentic and alternative assessment began between professionals whom we identify as 'assessment revolutionaries' and those representing the 'testing establishment.' However, since then, with assessment initiatives now implemented in many states, the public is awakening both to the problems and the promises of new forms of student assessment. At this point, considerable distance exists between what the public sector wants and what professional revolutionaries advocate concerning assessment reforms.

The terms alternative assessment and authentic assessment are used interchangeably, but do not mean the same thing. Typically, the idea of authentic assessment is that human knowledge is created in human activity. These activities are necessary to solve real-life problems within a local or community context. Designers of authentic assessments create tasks that confront children with open-ended realistic problems. While solving these problems, children show how they construct meaning and apply knowledge in a particular setting to achieve results. On the other hand, the idea of alternative assessment suggests that human learning is complex and knowledge is multidimensional in the forms it takes. Professionals need different forms of assessment to represent the complexity of human learning. Advocates suggest that alternative measures of student attainment which legitimize multiple modes of assessment will be more respectful of human diversity, give a more accurate picture of student skills and abilities, and provide alternatives to standardized measures of student attainment.

For many professionals, the press toward authentic and alternative assessment is a bold and necessary school initiative. Since the progressive reforms of the 1960s, no school reform has focused more centrally on the nature of the teaching and learning process, nor has any restructuring initiative held more tenaciously to the importance of increased teacher capacity to increase student outcomes. Taken at face value, the

0268–0939/97 $12 · 00 © 1997 Taylor & Francis Ltd.

alluring and highly rational logic of driving instructional change through improved assessment sounds preeminently sensible. It removes the clutter of indirect social, economic, and environmental variables from the school achievement equation and focuses directly on instructional effectiveness to deliver outcomes.

In this chapter we discuss how alternative and authentic assessment reforms are shaped in the context of professional and public debate. We explore differences between professional and public views of assessment and discuss assessment reforms as they may influence children's achievement. We build this discussion around the public debate regarding California's full-circle experience with a high-profile state-wide initiative.

Professional revolutionaries and assessment reform

Advocating that authentic assessments are 'tests worth taking', revolutionary Grant Wiggins seeks to disenfranchise and vilify 'old guard testing-types' who claim that standardized tests are useful measures of student achievement (1993). Authentic, alternative, performance-based, on-demand, portfolio, curriculum-embedded, exhibitions, group projects, journals, teacher-observed, open-ended, essay-prompted assessments are but a few of the 'new' recommended forms of student evaluation. Understanding the politics of the debate between 'old guard' psychometricians and new views represented by cognitive psychologists is important as reformers attempt to shift claims of expertise from traditional psychometricians, their testing practices and instruments to new forms of assessments. Reformers seek to empower teachers and professional insiders as the new experts and to legitimize instruments that more closely represent the school and community context. Part of the intellectual debate involves an important shift in the discipline of psychology from behaviorism to psychological constructivism.

Phillips (1995) suggests that psychological constructivism has become 'something akin to a secular religion'. Constructivists are, by definition, subject oriented and claim that individuals do not come into the world with prestocked knowledge and preformulated structures for inquiry and cognition. Recent contributions from cognitive research show that individuals *construct knowledge* using subjective intellectual processes. This point is an important one in the assessment argument. Alignment with psychological constructivist views moves the site of knowledge production as internal to learners. It redirects the relationship of the context in which knowledge is produced. Constructivists claim that knowledge produced by students on standardized tests is a fragmented and decontextualized form of knowing. Not only is this knowledge not meaningful, it is a distorted picture of true achievement. Therefore, constructivist revolutionaries decry assessments of static forms of knowledge and preestablished models of inquiry. At the same time they seek legitimacy for dynamic, often messier, assessments of complex intellectual processes and knowledge generated in these contexts.

Taking a more moderate position from extremely subjective views of knowledge, Moss (1996) suggests that the interpretivists make a contribution to the assessment debate which pulls intellectual thought into the foreground. Due to a focus on *how* meaning develops in context, interpretivists see human knowledge as intersubjective and socially constructed. Most argue that traditional psychometric measurement, with its naturalist conception of science, cannot capture complex phenomena.

A more subtle, but important part of the intellectual debate about assessment is about power. From a social critical perspective, reformers seek representation of the subject's domain of knowledge as a legitimate form of knowing. Over-reliance on efficient psychometric measures of school achievement gives no credence to the subjective or intersubjective experiences of the learner. As a matter of course, it is precisely that voice that psychometrics excludes in objective views of measuring knowledge. Though new cognitivist, interpretivist, and social critical views of assessment can be mutually exclusive, most reformers work between extremes, seeing alternative and authentic forms of assessing student achievement as offering a wider range of good assessment practices.

An emerging shift in professional debates may be a willingness, on the part of the external 'testing establishment', to experiment with ways to assess intersubjective forms of knowledge. With increased legitimacy of this domain of testing, schools may be able to account for important school and student outcomes which have been downplayed in the past.

Alternative assessment in the broad context of school reform

Early proponents of alternative assessments envisioned the reform as a 'grass roots' mandate from professional and parent communities alike. Advocates sought to empower parents and teachers with meaningful information concerning children's progress toward important educational goals. In the broader context of school reform and restructuring debates, what emerges is the incorporation of some ideologies of early assessment reforms and not others. Key ideas presented in national- and state-level discussions represent a streamlined and idealized view of how the standard setting and assessment processes should work to restructure schools. A few of the most salient ideas are discussed here to illuminate the national dialogue.

The standard setting process: One promise of democratic responsiveness in school reforms is 'the standard setting process'. Setting standards for student performance is often preceded by values exercises by which a community attempts to clarify its preferences. A typical discussion begins with the most popular question of reform rhetoric, 'What should all students know and be able to do'? Ideally, through a democratic collaborative process, communities draft educational standards from prioritized values. Models for standard setting are prescribed for a group of any size, level of governance, or political and professional persuasion. Most proponents of standard setting see local initiative as an essential part of reforms to reengage community interest in schools. However, as O'Neil (1992) suggests, much of the political thrust for standard setting comes from a feeling that education needs a stronger presence at the national level. Whether used to engage community-, state- or national-level interest in educational dialogue, there is little doubt that standard setting is a valuable tool for legitimizing the goals of public education.

The standards and the tests: A dual political shift captures the call for excellence and high standards in educational reform. The first shift advocates for developing a set of standards *all* students must achieve. This displaces accepting a standardized view of achievement where some children excel and others fail as an expected result of normal distribution of achievement. The second shift suggests that all tests ought to be instructionally sound and material tested ought to be made explicit to teacher and learner. This requires developing a set of tests that are both worth teaching to and worthy of students' preparation (Wiggins 1993).

Like Jaime Escalante's success at teaching to the Advanced Placement Calculus exam, many teachers find the idea of standards appealing. Standards pin down public intent about what curriculum teachers ought to teach and set out the criteria for evaluation so teachers can aim students at fixed targets. For the moment, the shift to standards appears equally persuasive to both professional and public sectors.

As a political phenomenon, the extraordinary appeal of standards lies in the common-sense logic of the concept itself. In public life, the idea of a 'standard' is not new or complex. Most industries articulate standards for product performance. Standards can be low or high; for instance, an egg can be rated with indicators of freshness as a 'Grade A' to 'Grade AAA'. A product or performance meeting the standard requires the application of a valued and explicit set of criteria and a judge who says, 'yes' or 'no'. For the public, the adoption of standards sets goals and gives a sense of direction for school work and the standards, themselves, acquire the weight of endorsed public policy.

Systemic change through coordinated assessments: Educational change theorist, Fullan, argues that goals should be monitored by 'inbuilt' assessments and feedback systems designed to diagnose and direct continuous positive educational change (1991). In this sense, ongoing assessment of student work provides the critical information to such a feedback system. Resnick and Tucker, leaders of a national assessment project, possess a vision of assessment reform as the primary 'catalyst' for systemic restructuring. They see a system where state and district partners are working with a cluster of specialists – learning and teaching researchers, curriculum specialists, assessment and testing experts, staff development professionals, and leaders in systemic education reform – to design and implement a system of performance standards, authentic assessments and professional development intended to change the way the American school system works (Simmons and Resnick 1993).

In her essay 'The politics of coherence' (1993), Fuhrman advocates a new role for policy makers that suggests following a national 'voluntaristic' path to school reform. Legislators would legitimize standard-setting entities, such as the National Council of Teachers of Mathematics (NCTM) and support 'consensus-reaching' structures to advance national goals at all levels of school governance. Standards and assessments would focus on a 'streamlined' body of knowledge and skills increasingly called 'the new basics'. Politicians would be challenged to produce consensus and coherence rather than negotiating for special interests.

School delivery standards: An important focus of broader restructuring initiatives is whether reforms can produce both equal access *and* equal outcomes for students whom the school system has traditionally underserved. Porter (1993) and Darling-Hammond (1994) suggest educational equity is achieved in assessment reforms by developing 'opportunity to learn' standards. These school delivery standards hold school leaders accountable for providing increased access to learning opportunities for *all parties* directly involved in assessments. Advocates suggest that school delivery standards are the key link between setting high standards and actualizing high student attainment. It is patently unfair, they argue, to hold teachers and students accountable for knowledge and skills that they have not been given a fair opportunity to learn.

Thus, a commitment to building teachers' capacity to maximize learning is a key link in reform.

If assessment reform is taken seriously and not as a palliative at treatment for poor and minority youth, then the implication for redistribution of public resources based on open access and standard expected outcomes is profound. Public commitment to educating *all capable youth to a set level* would be severely tested and the equalizing function of American schooling more fully realized.

Multiple assessments and accounts of school work: Accountability in education is a politically responsive phrase used to address public sector needs for explanations of school results. New forms of assessment that offer multiple and more complex views of school achievement are proving uniquely flexible as tools for accountability. Portfolios, for instance, are increasingly used as tools for parent conferencing, whereas performance-based assessments based on standards, for instance, writing standards, may be used for evaluating program delivery and instructional effectiveness.

Proponents of increased accountability for public schools suggest that account giving will increase school effectiveness. Similar to economic models of organization, this view assumes that the public knows what it wants and will hold school officials responsible for results. Here, increased and varied assessment should guarantee attainment. However, institutional theorists Meyer and Rowan (Powell and DiMaggio 1991) claim that schools are public institutions and their organization is different from economic models of organization. They suggest that increased accountability may increase the social legitimacy of public schools and justify their existence without directly affecting achievement.

However, Palmer–Wolf, LeMahieu, and Eresh (1992) offer a different view of the possible function of alternative assessments and their relationship to accountability. They see high standards and assessments as tools for producing a new kind and level of school accountability. Arguing that it is important to distinguish between assessments of the 'enacted' curriculum as internal accounts and tests of the 'official' curriculum as external accounts, they think that alternative assessments could encourage more honest internal accounts of student growth. This would press professionals, internally, toward greater equity in delivery of achievement.

In national debates, assessment initiatives respond to the public sense of our 'nation at risk' as we seek to reduce uneasiness about poor education. What emerges in the political dialogue is a streamlined rational linear view of how to solve the problem of school structures that inhibit achievement. By pinning down goals, the field of necessary attainment is narrowed. With continuous assessments using explicit criteria, the operational shakedown is centered on irrational instruction. The search for equity centers on the internal organizing school principles and built in social biases that must change to give all children opportunities to learn. Thus far this smooth and compelling story is far from being achieved as there are many technical, political, and economic factors still in the way.

Parent and public views of assessment reforms

Recent public opinion research shows that although the US public has concerns about the status of public schools, overall, they support public schooling and hold similar broad-based educational goals for students (Johnson and Immerwahr 1994, Johnson *et al.* 1995). For instance, the public rates basic skills such as reading, writing, basic mathematics, and computer competence, in addition to responsibility and self-discipline, as fundamental goals for student achievement.

However, as broad goals are operationalized and content is further defined, the consensus breaks down. For example, in the Public Agenda reports cited above, 95% of Americans believed that it is important to teach students respect for others despite their racial or ethnic background. And 76% of Americans believed that teaching students about the African-American struggle for civil rights in the 1950s and 1960s is important. However, 44% of the public believed that teaching that racism is the main cause of the economic and social problems African–Americans face today is highly inappropriate.

In relation to assessment, parents report that they value conversations with teachers that provide relevant and specific information about their child's educational progress (Anderson and Bachor 1993, Diffily 1993). Parents rate talking with teachers and seeing graded examples of children's work as the most useful for understanding academic progress (Shepard and Bleim 1993). In one study, Shepard and Bleim (1993) showed parents samples of both multiple-choice items and performance tasks. Parents approved of both, but preferred the performance tasks, especially in reading. Even parents who favored using standardized tests valued performance tasks used to improve instruction. In fact, researchers report that parents' examination of the actual assessments was educative. Parental doubts faded as they examined the performance assessments, observing that they seemed hard, challenging, and thought provoking for students. However, parents express serious concerns about the transferability of new assessment and reporting formats, such as narratives, and their child's eventual preparedness for college entrance exams (Diffily 1993).

Past reform efforts have negatively affected public response and the public has a different sense of urgency about assessment reforms from professionals. Though many states are continuing down the path of assessment reform, California's initiative provides clear instances of the distance between public and professional views concerning assessment and reveals important tensions inherent in reforms.

California's CLAS(-sic) case: assessment reform: Been there, done that . . .

As early as the mid-1980s, California's existing statewide testing system reflected a greater use of performance assessments in Language Arts and Mathematics. In 1991, the Legislature and Governor Deukmejian mandated the development of the California Learning Assessment System (CLAS) through Senate Bill 662. CLAS relied heavily on performance tasks that reflected the California Curriculum Frameworks and recommendations of the National Council of English and Mathematics and of the Mathematics Sciences Education Board, which stress problem-solving and communication (Cronbach *et al.* 1994). Progressive professionals and political supporters of the legislation viewed the new assessments and associated performance standards as crucial lever to implement state curriculum initiatives. The CLAS tasks were to serve as models for teachers to develop classroom assessments and to drive instruction towards desired change. Performance standards were to raise expectations for student perfomance by communicating to teachers, students, parents, and the community the essential criteria for 'good' performance and what students needed to accomplish (CLAS 1993, Rothman 1995).

In 1993, CLAS was administered to fourth-, eighth-, and tenth-grade students in reading, writing, and mathematics. Although the 1993 administration was considered a 'practice run', the state department of education released a public report of results. School officials had access to extensive materials to help parents and community groups better understand CLAS. Yet a review of these materials revealed a lack of information regarding the measurement error associated with the new test results (Cronbach *et al.* 1994). If performance was low, parents and communities had no way to judge the accuracy of scores. When schools that had generally done well on standardized tests did poorly on CLAS, there was gossip that performance levels had been arbitrarily scaled. Some professionals felt low scores were a 'set up' to convey a sense of crisis and increase pressure on schools. Additionally, comparison groups used to report school-level results obscured rather than highlighted differences in performance. Clear comparisons among school groups, which related to community factors, could have provided a stimulus for broader-based societal reforms. However, political consideration, rather than expert advice, governed decisions on technical and public reporting issues that later proved problematic. Additionally, legislators, test makers, and school professionals quickly became challenged by the public criticisms and parent activism.

The materials and context of some assessment tasks challenged fundamental beliefs of certain constituencies. Charging that the story was anti-religion, Conservative Christians and other parent groups objected to the use of a reading passage involving a young African-American Christian women about to marry an African-American Muslim man.

Newspapers published reports of technical concerns over the validity and reliability of the test administration. Reports carried in the *Los Angeles Times* and the conservative *Orange County Press-Enterprise* echoed concerns reported by a Select Committee which reviewed technical problems with the test (Cronbach *et al.* 1994). With public confusion over the competence of state-level technical experts and conservative groups, such as the Traditional Values Coalition (TVC), exposing the 'decadent' values expressed in the literature selections, resistance to the exams was building. Adding fuel to the fire, the State Department of Education refused to allow anyone to preview the tests. Additionally, they stuck to a mandate that all children take the tests so, as a result, the TVC and the Rutherford group offered free legal assistance to any parent or group wishing to fight these demands. Smart political oppositionists linked the CLAS exams with the building controversy over 'values embedded' Outcomes-Based-Education, which they branded as a leftist reform. Soon the controversy climaxed. Sponsoring SB 1273, State Senator Gary Hart, a leader in state education legislation, tried to bail out CLAS by renaming the system and seeking renewed funding for the reform. Acting like any astute politician in an election year, Governor Wilson vetoed the bill and subsequently scuttled the entire initiative. Within a few weeks the entire CLAS office was gone. Officials called on to carry on the state assessment burden were looking at old standardized tests and scratching their heads. Legislators introduced a new law that mandates valid, reliable, and standardized measures. . .along with other assessments. In a matter of three to four years of high-energy and high-stakes activity, California's initiative had been won and lost.

Emerging public response to assessment reforms

Consensus, but at what level?: Analysis of assessment reforms reveals a symbolic concentration of political power, e.g. broad goal-setting initiatives, in favor of state and national control. Standard-setting processes that produce agreement on national assessments through professional and policy maker efforts are both a rationalizing force and a recentering force for legitimizing state interest in American schools. While the crisis of national disunity and ill ease about the mission of public education might be resolved by national consensus, the tension between local community leadership and state authority over educational goals and assessment may increase. Many school districts have decentralized authority to local decision-making entities and worked toward direct and responsive forms of leadership. With enhanced rights many local communities have set goals and developed assessments responsive to local concerns. A conundrum for community action to support national goals is that the extent to which goals overlap between national and community interests is the extent to which tensions and conflicts are reduced. But overlap of goals blurs community boundaries and local differentiation seen as necessary to sustain local commitment to education.

Content issues?: No test is value-free. However, some, like norm-referenced tests, are politically legitimized and the content appears neutral and stable to the public. In the California case, the control of content selection by professional liberals reflected the bias typical of this group. The exclusion of voices from right-wing groups, such as the Traditional Values Coalition, disenfranchised their right to decide whether sacred values were violated by content choices. Experts might have avoided controversy over the values embedded in literary selections earlier but conflict was certain when state officials used technical authority to deny parents access to the exams. It appears they shut the public out at the precise moment they needed to open the door and let the power of parent education and judgment assist reforms. Consequently, now the conservative press could frame the entire movement as a liberal conspiracy led by inept professional technicians who would 'get their way' despite public concerns.

Testing basics?: Professionals have distanced themselves from perennial public and parent concerns over testing for essential skills and knowledge. Here, the public and parent stance is clear. It is predictable that conflict over testing the 'basics' will continue. Though we can argue that new forms of assessments are intriguing and even interesting to parents, parents are concerned that their children receive the universal 'basics.' Newly revised standardized tests are a likely, but unintended, consequence of alternative assessment reforms.

Portability of test results?: Another serious concern for parents is the mismatch between forms of assessments used across institutions and levels. American schools are not connected in a national system that has direct authority over educational tests. Assessment reforms are not progressing in an even fashion. If children can use calculators on one test, but not another, then they are ill prepared when we teach them only with calculators. The Scholastic Aptitude Test continues to be a primary instrument used to sort students for college education. Until it is replaced, students must have experience with this type of assessment and learn the content and types of questions that are apt to be encountered on the exam.

Competition verses cooperation?: In the past, the public has trusted that standardized achievement tests measure some 'true' individually achieved school attainment. In part, alternative assessments contest this view and offer more subtle and complex views of student achievement, but Americans value the spirit of 'fair' and 'blind' competitive measures of individual effort. Revolutionaries are naive to think that the power of public norms, which favor competitive forms of assessment, will be thrown aside.

It is also true that Americans value cooperation but not on tests of individual achievement. When conservative factions evaluate reforms which suggest that individuals could suffer with lower scores because group cooperation was poor, conflict over cooperative assessments of student achievement is certain. Conversely, when student portfolio work represents parent and teacher assistance, public concerns arise, not over the value of assistance, but over the assignment of individual scores to student achievement.

Finally, it is clear that most parents understand, at least intuitively, that children's learning is far more complex than current exams portray. No doubt, parents will continue to show interest in more individualist and self-determined views of assessment which provoke student imagination and critical thinking. However, there is little social history or tradition to support such assessments for widespread public use. In its current form, the science and art of alternative assessment is too new for broad public endorsement.

What emerges to inform policy?

Several years into the reform, *it is apparent that if alternative and authentic assessment was a grass-roots public reform, the grass was much greener inside the 'mind worlds' of professionals than it was in the 'life worlds' of the parents and the public.*

Technical concerns and real costs are different for authentic and alternative assessments from traditional assessments. New forms are still experimental and even if experiments are successful, more time is necessary to perfect technologies than was first conceptualized. Problems exist with respect to validity, reliability, timely feedback, aggregation and interpretation of results, and assignation of individual scores.

What emerges from this brief discussion is that assessment policies need to respect traditional public norms and values while at the same time addressing concerns of professionals. Teachers are concerned about distortion of instruction caused by excessive pressure to do well on standardized tests. Teaching to 'tests worth taking', holding to fixed standards, and developing meaningful and useful measures of student achievement is an area of public policy which has been neglected. However, new forms of assessment need to allow time for the public to gain experience with them and may need to accommodate conflicting private values or offer parent options.

Finally, it appears that once again the concept of a revolutionary change to fix public schools is not the means to this end. Using tests as 'shock treatment' to force the school system to change is likely to be unsuccessful, wasteful and mean spirited. In California's case, a sense of mass failure on the first round of alternative assessment reporting probably did more to demoralize teachers and confuse the public than it did to support change. Assessment reforms which allow adaptation and capacity building on the part of all parties may produce better end results. The least understood potential in the movement is the development of national assessments. It is too early to tell how a system of coordinated assessments might look on a grand scale. Certainly it would be interesting experiment.

Will assessment reforms enhance children's worlds?

The extraordinary *energy* of assessment conversations suggests the whole issue needs serious attention. No doubt as cognitive science evolves, new forms of assessment will allow a more dynamic and accurate profile of student performance. As a better picture of student learning processes emerges, so will the picture alter traditional views of student capacity and development. Authentic assessments as intersubjective or community-based forms of knowing have potential for honoring individual ways of knowing and enhancing the value of schooling as a community experience. In new ways, this may decrease student alienation from school and promote their sense of inclusion in a local, immediate, and personal world. Additionally, validating students' subjective experiences have the potential for increasing self-knowledge and self-worth.

However, regardless of the positive effects of assessment reform, little research confronts the possible downside effects of increased assessments. Test takers feel stress, and a child's sense of stress at their inability to meet standards may tax their personal capacity to integrate failure. This issue needs to be discussed and understood. New forms of assessment and accountability place greater responsibility on students. It would seem that sensitivity to inappropriate uses of assessment and assignment of blame for failure could have devastating consequences in local or communal forms of assessment. Failure on external measures is impersonal and can be discounted by the student. Unless students see new assessments as enhancing and promoting their educational experience, they may experience further alienation from school.

As the public and professional sectors call for increased accountability, using assessments as a means to match intents with outcomes, finding a balance which directly protects and promotes children's interests in their own educational futures needs to be carefully considered.

References

ANDERSON, J. O. and BACHOR, D. G. (1993) Assessment practices in the elementary classroom: perspectives of stake-holders. Paper presented at the annual meeting of the National Council on Measurement in Education, Atlanta, GA.

CALIFORNIA LEARNING ASSESSMENT SYSTEM OFFICE (1993) California Learning Assessment System: a development and implementaion plan for 1993–94. Report submitted to the Department of Finance

CRONBACH, L. L., BRADBURN, N. M. and HORVITZ, D. G. (1994) Sampling and statistical procedures used in the California Learning Assessment System. Report of Select Committee to the Acting State Superintendent of Public Instruction.

DARLING-HAMMOND, L. (1994) Performance-based assessment and educational equity. *Harvard Educational Review*, **64**(1).

DIFFILY, D. (1993) What parents think about alternative assessment and narrative reporting: one school's findings. Technical report. ERIC No. ED 381230.

FUHRMAN, S. H. (ed.) (1993) *Designing Coherent Education Policy: Improving The System* (San Francisco: Jossey-Bass).

FULLAN, M. G. (1991) *The New Meaning Of Educational Change*, 2nd edn (New York: Teachers College Press).

JOHNSON, J. FARKAS, S., FRIEDMAN, W., IMMERWAHR, J. and BERS, A. (1995) *Assignment Incomplete: The Unfinished Business Of Educational Reform* (New York: Public Agenda).

JOHNSON, J. and Immerwahr, J. (1994) *First Things First: What Americans Expect From Public Schools* (New York: Public Agenda).

Moss, P. A. (1996) Enlarging the dialogue in educational measurement: voices from interpretive research traditions. *Educational Researcher*, **25**(1).

O'Neil, J. (1992) Putting performance assessment to the test. *Educational Leadership*, **49**(8).

Palmer-Wolf, D., LeMahieu, P. Eresh, J. (1992) Good measure: assessment as a tool for educational reform. *Educational Leadership*, **49**(8).

Phillips, D. C. (1995) The good, the bad and the ugly: the many faces of constructivism. *Educational Researcher*, **24**(7).

Porter, A. C. (1993) School delivery standards. *Educational Researcher*, **22**(5).

Powell, W. W. and DiMaggio, P. J. (1991) *The New Institutionalism In Organizational Analysis* (Chicago, IL: University of Chicago Press).

Rothman, R. (1995) *Measuring Up: Standards, Assessment, And School Reform* (San Francisco, CA: Jossey-Bass).

Shepard, L. A. and Bleim, C. L. (1993) *Parent Opinions About Standardized Tests, Teacher's Information And Performance Assessment: A Case Study Of The Effects Of Alternative Assessment In Instruction, Student Learning And Accountability Practices* (Los Angeles, CA: CRESST).

Simmons, W. and Resnick, L. (1993) Assessment as the catalyst of school reform. *Educational Leadership*, **50**(5).

Wiggins, G. (1993) Assessment: authenticity, context, and validity. *Phi Delta Kappan*, **75**(3).

12.   Calling for community in a conservative age

Catherine A. Lugg
Rutgers University
New Brunswick, New Jersey

Within the profession of American education, there has been a movement towards embracing various notions of 'critical pedagogy' in the hopes of revitalizing fragile communities, especially in urban areas. Heartened by a possibly neo-progressive approach towards education, teachers, administrators, and especially academicians are exploring once again what it means to be an educated citizen in an increasingly heterogeneous democratic republic. Words such as 'community', 'critical', and 'empowerment', while at times ill-defined, abound in the professional literature. There appears to be growing professional consensus that public education should inculcate the values of tolerance, understanding, and an appreciation of difference: seemingly uncontroversial norms considered vital to the health of democracy.

Much of this recent pedagogical work has been grounded in the tenets of critical theory, or the Frankfurt School (Hlebowitsh 1992). Critical pedagogy, an intellectual descendant, is specifically concerned with power and oppression and how they are made manifest within a given society. It examines and critiques how certain cultural groups learn to accept, engage in, and/or resist oppression as transmissed through the public schools and that broader society (Giroux 1983). Such a focus is, of course, educational. Critical pedagogy also contains immediate and profound political implications. If public education is to develop 'critical thinkers' who engage and dissect (deconstruct?) the myriad social constructions of 'reality', public education, in conjunction with like-minded individuals, has the potential of radically transforming the social and political landscape of the United States (Giroux 1992). If not explicitly a societal panacea (Perkinson 1991), public schooling might become a liberating tonic for historically marginalized groups, such as African and Hispanic Americans, poor people, gays and lesbians, to name just a few.

However, critical pedagogy fails to address the political depth and strength of the current dominant ideology, American conservative ideology. If schools of education are embracing one collection of political and educational ideals and their constituent symbols (i.e. critical pedagogy), the present political environment reflects quite another (i.e. American conservative ideology). It appears that a symbolic crusade is being waged for power and influence regarding the direction of US public education (Gusfield 1963), with professional educators and religious and political conservatives at philosophical loggerheads over what is meant by the term *community*. Additionally, schools of education appear to be strangely ill-equipped and unwilling to acknowledge their growing irrelevance in these increasingly rancorous political debates. Employing the methodologies of political historiography (Tuck 1991) and

0268–0939/97 $12 · 00 © 1997 Taylor & Francis Ltd.

historical policy analysis (Warren 1983, Silver 1990), this article examines the political tensions between American conservative ideology and critical pedagogy, and concludes by offering possible directions for future educational policy.

Critical pedagogy and conservative ideology

There are some fundamental perils involved in exploring two admittedly contentious political schools of thought. With the recent resurgence of the 'religious right', there is a danger of invoking certain easy stereotypes regarding conservative (and especially fundamentalist) Christians. Many of these simplistic rhetorical icons emerged during the Scopes 'monkey trial' of the 1920s, and quickly found their way into the larger social academic discourses (Livingstone 1987). Subsequently, educational scholars have tended to discount, sometimes snidely, the longevity, power and appeal of more overtly theological approaches towards American politics, and to public educational practices in particular.

This caution against easy stereotypes also applies when examining critical pedagogy, although for differing reasons. Thanks to the pioneering work of scholars such as Michael Apple, Henry Giroux and Peter McLaren, critical pedagogy has gained a considerable amount of intellectual cachet during the last decade, sometimes to the consternation of more traditional academics. There *is* a certain historical irony in that neo-Marxist analyses of public schooling are flourishing at a time when the odor of 'vulgar Marxist' political practices is fading in many parts of the world. But American academic traditionalists, in particular, have tended to underestimate the analytic and descriptive power of the various critical approaches, and subsequently critical pedagogy's political appeal for more agenda-oriented scholars. Perhaps, when examining either critical theory (or pedagogy) and Christianity (broadly defined and applied to American politics), academics of various disciplinary stripes should heed Cornel West's injunction (1982: 136), 'Stalinism is to Marxism what the Ku Klux Klan is to Christianity; a manipulation of the chief symbols yet diametrically opposed to the central values'. Scholars should dispense with ready-made allegations of bad faith toward both Christianity and Marxism.

Before moving into the heart of this philosophical exploration, some basic parameters also need to be established. This article is principally concerned with two central concepts within critical pedagogy and conservative ideology, and how these in turn might address similar political and social issues (both adherents would argue *moral* from profoundly differing standpoints. Critical pedagogy, like critical theory, concerns itself with hegemony and liberation, or how individuals contribute to, and/or are tacitly complicit in, their own and others' oppression, and how they (we?) in turn might work collectively in resisting. Conservative ideology, with its roots in both orthodox and fundamentalist Christianity (see Nash 1976, Himmelstein 1983, Gottfried 1993), is concerned with individual sin and how humanity might be better led towards redemption and eternal salvation. These notions are complex and seemingly have little to do with one another, yet it is how they are played out upon the stage of educational politics, and how they are or are not operationalized, that provides insights to the direction of future educational and social policies.

Critical pedagogy: hegemony and liberation

Much of critical pedagogy's concern with hegemony and resistance is grounded in the works of the Italian Marxist, Antonio Gramsci. Writing while imprisoned during Benito Mussolini's reign, Gramsci explored why a corrupt ruling class was able to remain in power and even maintain a high degree of popular support from those it oppressed (Gramsci 1971). Of particular interest to critical theorists and pedagogues is his theory of hegemony, or how the privileged group maintains power through various cultural and historical mechanisms (West 1982). Gramsci moved the analytical focus from state-imposed violence to insure the acquiescence of subordinated groups (i.e. the capitalist/proletariat struggle), to examining how consent is established and maintained, not imposed, through various educational processes (Burke 1992, Giroux 1992). Phrased differently, the concern is with how those in power legitimize their oppression through persuasion. As Cornel West explains (1982: 136):

> A hegemonic culture subtly and effectively encourages people to identify themselves with the habits, sensibilities, and world views supportive of the status quo and the class interests that dominate it. It is a culture successful in persuading people to 'consent' to their oppression and exploitation.

Viewed as such, hegemony is both a political and educational process; it is the pursuit of establishing a society's common sense. Yet, such consent is continually renegotiated. An individual might learn his/her proper place within the larger social order, but this 'place' is always contested ground.

It is during this contest where resistance to such notions of place may occur, and it is resistance that is a chief concern to critical pedagogy. If children are taught how to question, resist, and possibly reject conventional wisdom in exploring socially constructed boundaries of race, class, ethnicity, gender and orientation, then communities, and eventually society, might be transformed ending a given hegemonic regime. Instead of treating the examination of social oppression as a peripheral issue, it is moved to the centre of the educational enterprise (Burke 1992). As such, education can become a profoundly liberating experience, moving individuals from a subordinated and oppressed status to that of critically informed citizens within a democratic society.

In this contested arena, the politics of education and the politics of social policy are brought into sharper focus by critical pedagogues. Teachers, administrators and schools are inseparable from the larger political-critical pedagogues would argue cultural-sphere(s). These are not, and cannot be, neutral sites that merely impart academic knowledge to schoolchildren. Critical pedagogy views teaching as both a political and profoundly moral act, with radical teacher/educators reconceptualized as 'cultural workers' (Giroux 1992). In this light, teachers and administrators might be viewed as the ultimate politicized 'street-level bureaucrats' (Weatherly and Lipsky 1977), shaping curriculum for 'critical' ends.

One method of critical shaping, or of moving from periphery to centre, is to redefine history itself – where the only valid criterion is political serviceability – which is a fine tradition in US educational historiography (see Finkelstein 1992: 255–297). According to Giroux (1992: 242), 'Of primary importance for cultural workers is the need to resurrect traditions and social memories that provide a new way of reading history and reclaiming power and identity'. However, there is an immediate problem with this quasi-historical approach, *the fallacy of presentism*. As defined by David Hackett Fischer (1970: 135), presentism is 'the mistaken idea that the proper way to do history is to prune away the dead branches of the past, and to preserve the green buds and twigs that have grown into the dark forest of our contemporary world'. It is the highly selective sampling of past events (disregarding those which are ideologically inconvenient), for current utility. In their quest for community, the presentism of critical pedagogues can obscure historical political cleavages and struggles, not only between various oppressed groups, but within them.

Ironically, in searching history for answers, critical pedagogues are, perhaps, more similar to their conservative critics than they are probably comfortable in admitting. A selected use of the past is also a vital political strategy to conservative ideology, especially the social traditionalist strain (Nash 1976). Again, historic differences that are politically troublesome are neatly dispensed with, usually in the name of maintaining community and tradition.

Conservative ideology and social traditionalism: sin and redemption

Contemporary conservative ideology is composed of three diverse, and at times conflicting, strands of political thought: social traditionalism, economic libertarianism and militant anti-communism (Nash 1976, Himmelstein 1983, Gottfried 1993, Lugg 1996). 'Whereas libertarians concern themselves with various notions of economic and personal liberty, and anti-communists worry about the possible military machinations of socialist and communist countries, social traditionalists have historically focused upon the social and moral welfare of US society' (Boyd et al. 1996: 348). The moral condition of the broader American culture (or community) is the central domestic policy focus for traditionalists.

Like critical pedagogy, social traditionalism looks at the broader US social and cultural institutions, but traditionalists focus upon how these institutions provide a sense of community, continuity and order. Additionally, an imposed sense of community, as long as it conforms to their sense of 'tradition', is not particularly problematic.[1] Individuals are viewed as essentially corrupt and in need of moral regulation, yet state regulation is seen as potentially tyrannical, especially if the power for enforcing such regulation is held by those who hold profoundly differing ideological and/or theoretical ideals (see Farney 1996).

For social traditionalists, religion, especially as reflected by institutionalized Christianity, is paramount to insuring a just society (Nash 1976, Himmelstein 1983, Gottfried 1993). There is, of course, a danger of gross simplification. Not all devout Christians are social traditionalists, nor are all social traditionalists Christians (many are not). Social traditionalism is ultimately a political ideology, although it does have obvious theological underpinnings (Lugg 1996). Social traditionalism is, first and foremost, politically conservative, and it is explicitly antithetical to an older Christian tradition such as the Social Gospel which is politically progressive and reformist (Torbet 1950, Ahlstrom 1972, Nash 1976, Hudson 1981, Sykes and Booty 1988). The teachings of Christianity, with its messages of sin, punishment, and of eternal salvation (redemption), are central (Lugg 1996).

Social traditionalism tends to view social problems as arising from the moral failings of individuals (sin) rather than as evidence of possible flaws within the larger political, social and economic order (see Murray 1984). Accordingly, people live in poverty thanks to their flawed morality, women are discriminated against because they have deserted their natural roles as wives and mothers, and so forth (Vedlitz 1988). Government intervention to ameliorate the effects of societal inequity is seen not only as ineffective, but as actually triggering massive social pathologies, such as teenage pregnancy. A few of the more prominent policy entrepreneurs (i.e. Robert Rector of the Heritage Foundation) even emply biblical quotations such as 'those who do not work, shall not eat' to highlight their disdain for social welfare programs. In the view of social traditionalism, the social welfare can be best maintained by private agencies and charities, not the government.

As with critical pedagogy, social traditionalism is very concerned with history, but for differing political ends. Those institutions which have a documented past, especially religiously affiliated philanthropic societies, are the focus of social traditio- nalism's historiography. However, besides the fallacy of presentism (Fischer 1970), there are some additional ideological perils traditionalism faces when plumbing his- tory for answers for present-day dilemmas. Many American traditions and social institutions, if not explicitly liberal, are not particularly conservative (Nash 1976). Nor has the country experienced long periods of domestic tranquility. Yet, conserva- tive social theorists like to pretend life was homogeneous and orderly in the past (Lugg 1996). For example, in calling for a return of religion to the public schools (school prayer, Bible readings, etc.), advocates invoke the rubric of 'our Judeo- Christian heritage' as a means of building social stability and moral communities. They forget that such activities were used to 'Anglicize' non-Protestant immigrant children. These coerced and state-mandated religious practices occasionally triggered deadly uprisings such as the Philadelphia Bible riots of 1843, in which 13 people died and a Roman Catholic Church was destroyed (Kaestle 1983, Spring 1994, Bennett 1995).

Historically, social traditionalism has favored the role of public education and public school teachers as transmitting a vaguely defined Judeo-Christian heritage, with stronger focus upon the Christian than the Judeo (Carter 1993). The current calls for returning prayer and God to the American classroom, of scrapping multicul- tural and sex education, and of returning basic American values to US education, all invoke a sense of 'Paradise Lost'. Within social traditionalist rhetoric, there is a sense that the USA had a golden age of public education, where students were orderly and polite, eagerly engaged in the intellectual pursuit of Western Civilization, and that public schools were academically effective. While the foundations for such dis- cussions are, in part, rather mythical, they do hold a certain political appeal by tapping into a national mood of ongoing angst. However, unlike critical pedagogues, social traditionalists have been very effective in employing the politics of symbolism to shape the direction of educational policy (Boyd et al. 1996). This is especially impor- tant to the current debates regarding community building and public schools.

Ideology, theology and the politics of education

A central irony regarding current educational debates over community is that while critical pedagogy's US proponents have represented elite interests (and academics, despite vigorous protestations to the contrary, *are* socially, politically, and economic- ally elite), conservative political activists have focused on building local grass-roots and wider populist support for their own ideological agendas. On the local level, con- servative activists seem to be motivated by the narrowest strain of American conservative ideology, social traditionalism (Boyd *et al.* 1996), and have been aided in some locations by their local Chistian Coalition. Social traditionalists, using specific and accessible campaign strategies such as 'marketing your message' (seee Hertsgaard 1988), have been very successful in getting out the vote favoring their own educational and social policy agendas.

On the other hand, critical pedagogues have largely limited their activism to the academy, ignoring the fact that state legislatures and local school boards have enormous influences upon classroom practices. Additionally, some critical pedagogues have adopted an almost impenetrable linguistic style, *à la* postmodernism, to differentiate between those who are in their academic 'club' and who are not (Ettinger 1994). From a grossly operational point of view, critical pedagogues' strategy seems doomed to failure, for it is the social traditionalists who have a much better sense of American grass-roots politics and the legislature's ear.

The explicit focus upon religion and the American sense of Christianity also provides social traditionalists with enormous political power (Carter 1993). Religious conservatives, in particular, have been extremely effective in mobilizing poor and working-class whites, a constituency for which critical theorists could claim a certain degree of sympathy owing to their economic oppression. Yet given critical pedagogues' neo-Marxist leanings and a certain disdain for religiosity, especially Christian fundamentalism (see Kincheloe 1993: 50–51), they and their critical educational agenda represent an anathema not only to most conservatives, but to a fair number of liberals and progressives as well. The latter may not object to the political ends envisioned by critical pedagogy, but are deeply troubled by the means.

In contrast, traditionalists, and specifically religious conservatives, have been unusually effective in employing powerful religious symbolism to highlight the discontent felt by many Americans of faith regarding public policy and the seemingly vacuous political sphere, or, 'the powerful sense of an America spinning out of control in ways that are, for many religious people, profoundly threatening' (Carter 1993: 264). While Americans of differing faiths disagree with their subsequent political agenda, they do share many of the same concerns (Lugg 1996).

The new religious right has also been effective in addressing the ill-ease felt by many Americans over the ever-shifting social mores and lack of economic stability (Phillips 1990, Coontz 1992). In charging that America is being (and will be) punished for supposedly renouncing its moral and religious foundations, both the religious and political right have brilliantly exploited the Christian notion of sin (Boyd *et al.* 1996). By subsequently offering a political strategy tailored at redeeming their definition of lost morality in a 'Christian nation', complete with a list of 'sinners' (secular humanists, single mothers, feminists, misguided liberals, teachers' unions, gays and lesbians, etc.), the religious right appeals to the Christian sense that individuals would rather feel guilty, when disaster strikes, then helpless (see Pagels 1988: 146). Many manifestations of the new religious right are very adept at exploiting the notion that woe only befalls evil-doers or those who countenance evil. Since many Americans have suffed real declines in their standard of living since the mid-1970s (Tyson 1986, Phillips 1990), such rhetoric provides a sense of human agency to individuals who, in fact, have little. It is far easier to accept that one chose badly (or that the country has fallen into sin) than to contemplate the possibility of powerlessness.

Ironically, given their explicit concern with the broader culture, religion has been critical pedagogues' ideological blind spot. While some have acknowledged its potential power (West 1982, Hooks 1993), very few critical scholars have explored religion

as a cultural and political artifact, why it could be a force of liberation, or more specifically, its enduring influence upon educational policy (for an exception, see
McLaren and Smith 1989). Like their non-critical academic compatriots, critical pedagogues have maintained a discreet distance from examining religion and its possible
influence upon public schools. There has also been a general professional assumption
within colleges of education that public schools have successfully disentangled themselves from religion. Technically, there have been stricter notions of separation of
church and state, beginning in 1962, with the Supreme Court voiding school prayer
in Engel v. Vitale (see Yudof *et al.* 1992). However, organized religion, especially as
manifested by conservative Christianity, has continued to exert a considerable inf-
lence upon US public schooling. The ongoing debate in Pennsylvania regarding
Outcome-Based Education is one recent example of organized religion's power in
directing education policy (Boyd *et al.* 1996).

The current question of what is meant by *community* (and exactly who is to be
included and, more troubling, excluded) quickly breaks down as critical pedagogy's
supporters sing to their admittedly small choir of like-minded academicians, while
conservative and religious activists mobilize the countryside. In the political contests
over public education critical pedagogy's proponents have not fared well. It is the
social traditionalists, not the critical pedagogues, that have achieved a measure of success in influencing both local and state educational policy and, subsequently, defining
community.

Public education, community, and symbolic crusades

The rise of the Christian Coalition and its fielding of school board candidates, coupled
with the political durability of other religious conservatives, has profound implications at both state and local governmental levels. This development is particularly
acute in the area of public school policy. The politics of schooling can function as a
lens, highlighting and magnifying parental and community anxieties regarding the
future of our children (see McCarthy 1994). Thanks to the long-term economic
anxiety, educational reform can quickly be transformed into symbolic crusades
(Gusfield 1963) and/or political spectacles (Edelman 1985, 1988).

Perhaps the most fractious political fights have been over Outcome-Based
Education (OBE) (Zahorchak 1994) and the movement towards systemic school
reform (Dryfoos 1994, Lugg 1994). Those opposing sweeping educational reforms
have tended to couch their opposition as 'standing up for traditional morality'
(Dryfoos 1994, Zahorchak 1994). The language of social traditionalists has been
highly symbolic (Lugg 1996), invoking a sense of loss (sin) and redemption, and on
occasion, it has been deliberately incendiary. For example, during the effort to pass
OBE in Pennsylvania, the outcomes listed under the category of 'appreciating and
understanding others' were quickly transformed by opponents into teaching public
school children to become homosexual. It was a blatant canard, but the charge was
highly effective in placing OBE's supporters on the defensive and it easily distorted
the entire issue of reform (Lugg and Boyd 1996).

Yet, there are important reasons for using public school reform (and the current
debates surrounding community) as means of furthering a specific political agenda,
which may or may not be connected to the matter at hand. As Joseph Gusfield long
ago noted (1963: 11):

> Since governmental actions symbolize the position of groups in the status structure, seeming ceremonial or ritual acts of government are often of great importance to many social groups. Issues which seem foolish or impractical items are often important for what they symbolize about the style or culture which is being recognized or derogated. Being acts of deference or degradation, the individual finds in governmental action that his own perceptions of his status in the society are confirmed or rejected.

Those who feel alienated from the power structure can be mobilized when seemingly mundane governmental procedures are perceived as threatening strongly held beliefs. The resulting political spectacle has the potential to reshape the issues involved with educational reform beyond all recognition. According to the political scientist Murray Edelman (1988: 96):

> The spectacle, in short, is a partly illusory parade of threats and reassurances, most of which have little bearing upon the successes and ordeals people encounter in their everyday lives, and some of which create problems that would not otherwise occur. The political spectacle does not promote accurate expectations or understanding, but rather evokes a drama that objectifies hopes and fears.

Social traditionalists' adept use of common American symbolism to recast individual differences and/or the process of change as sin (see Vedlitz 1988), puts critical pedagogues at a distinct cultural disadvantage when engaging in the politics of education. Critical pedagogues might 'win' the hearts of a number of teachers and administrators, but social traditionalists have proved to be highly effective at mobilizing the larger community in getting their candidates elected to school boards, and to state and federal offices. Subsequently, those elected officials involved with shaping public education policy may or may not be able to draw a picture when critical pedagogues discuss 'hegemony and oppression'. But most politicians, and Americans in general, can easily conjure various visions of 'sin'. In the realm of symbolic politics, social traditionalists have, perhaps, the most potent symbol when discussing future educational policies.

Whither community?

What are the implications for colleges of education, educators and their latest quest for *community*? First and foremost, building community through the public schools has been and will continue to be politically divisive (Wirt and Kirst 1992). Defining community and determining who belongs and who doesn't are contentious political issues (again, both critical pedagogues and social traditionalists would argue *moral*. Scholars of various disciplinary schools need to be cognizant of the difficulties involved with such undertakings and the host of complex dilemmas community building engenders.

Secondly, the political symbolism involved with public schooling and public school reform needs to be more closely examined. In particular, with the rise of conservative policy entrepreneurs, educational reform is even more of a politicized process, with a host of easy (if not corny) cultural condensation symbols pulled like rabbits from think-tankers' hats and tossed into a boiling political stew. Educational policy makers have tended to underestimate the power of 'symbolic crusades' and have subsequently been politically blind-sided by social traditionalists during the effort to pass various reforms (Dryfoos 1994, Boyd *et al.* 1996).

Finally, educational scholars need to re-examine the political influence of religion (not only conservative Christianity) upon the process of educational policy making, for the politics of US public education is a dynamic and volatile process. While it is explicable, the politics of eduation may not be particularly rational (Lugg 1996), nor perhaps should it be viewed as such (Lindblom and Woodhouse 1993). For those committed to strengthening public attention, a reexamination of religion in American public life is in order. There are powerful and disconcerting cultural reasons for American conservative ideology's political longevity that must be explored if one is to be 'critically engaged' in shaping educational policy.

Note

1. For example, conservative commentator William F. Buckley called for the represssion of Dr Martin Luther King, viewing both King and the civil rights movement as a direct threat to tradition (1968: 137). 'Repression is an unpleasant instrument, but it is absolutely necessary for civilizations that believe in order and human rights. I wish to God Hitler and Lenin had been repressed. And word should be gently got through to the nonviolent avengers that in the unlikely even that they succeed in mobilizing their legions, they will be most efficiently, indeed most zestfully, repressed. In the name, quite properly, of social justice.'

References

AHLSTROM, S. E. (1972) *A Religious History of the American People* (New Haven: Yale University Press).

BENNETT, D. H. (1995) *The Party of Fear: The American Far Right from Nativism to the Militia Movement* (New York: Vintage Books).

BOYD, W. L., LUGG, C. A., and ZAHORCHAK, G. L. (1996, May) Social traditionalists, religious conservatives and the politics of outcome-based education: Pennsylvania and beyond. *Education and Urban Society*, **28**(3), 347–365.

BUCKLEY, JR, W. F. (1968) *The Jeweler's Eye: A Book of Irresistible Political Reflections* (New York: Putman).

BURKE, P. (1992) *History and Social Theory* (Ithaca: Cornell University Press).

CARTER, S. L. (1993) *The Culture of Disbelief: How American Law and Politics Trivialize Religious Devotion* (New York: Doubleday).

COONTZ, S. (1992) *The Way We Never Were: American Families and the Nostalgia Trap* (New York: Basic Books).

DRYFOOS, J. G. (1994) *Full-Service Schools: A Revolution in Health and Social Services for Children, Youth, and Families* (San Francisco: Jossey-Bass).

EDELMAN, M. (1985) *The Symbolic Uses of Politics* (Urbana: University of Illinois Press).

EDELMAN, M. (1988) *Constructing the Political Spectacle* (Chicago: University of Chicago Press).

ETTINGER, M. (1994) The Pocahontas paradigm, or would the subaltern please shut up? in L. Garber (ed.), *Tilting The Tower* (New York: Routledge), 51–55.

FARNEY, D. (1996, January 30) Culture of faith: for Kansas' Freidlines, life politics, religion are mostly inseparable. *Wall Street Journal*, **227**(21), A1, A10.

FINKELSTEIN, B. (1992) Education historians as mythmakers, in G. Grant (ed.), *Review of Research in Education*, 18 (Washington: American Educational Research Association), 255–297.

FISCHER, D. H. (1970) *Historians' Fallacies: Towards a Logic of Historical Thought* (New York: Harper Torchbooks).

GIROUX, H. A. (1983) *Theory and Resistance in Education: A Pedagogy for the Opposition* (New York: Bergin & Garvey).

GIROUX, H. A. (1992) *Border Crossings: Cultural Workers and the Politics of Education* (New York: Routledge).

GOTTFRIED, P. (1993) *The Conservative Movement*, revised edn (New York: Twayne).

GRAMSCI, A. (1971) *Selections from the Prison Notebooks*, eds Q. Hoare and G. Nowell-Smith (New York: International Publishers).

GUSFIELD, J. R. (1963) *Symbolic Crusade: Status Politics and the American Temperance Movement* (Urbana: University of Illinois Press).

HERTSGAARD, M. (1988) *On Bended Knee: The Press and the Reagan Presidency* (New York: Farrar, Straus, Giroux).

HIMMELSTEIN, J. L. (1983) The new right, in R. C. Liebman and R. Wuthnow (eds), *The New Christian Right: Mobilization and Legitimation* (New York: Aldine), 15–30.

HLEBOWITSH, P. S. (1992) Critical theory versus curriculum theory: reconsidering the dialogue on Dewey. *Educational Theory*, **42**(1), 69–82.

HOOKS, B. (1994) *Teaching to Transgress: Education as the Practice of Freedom* (New York: Routledge).

HUDSON, W. S. (1981) *Religion in America*, 3rd edn (New York: Charles Scribner's Sons).

KAESTLE, C. F. (1983) *Pillars of the Republic: Common Schools and American Society, 1780–1960* (New York: Hill & Wang).

KINCHELOE, J. L. (1993) *Toward a Critical Politics of Teacher Thinking: Mapping the Postmodern* (Westport: Bergin & Garvey).

LIEBMAN, R. C. and WUTHNOW, R. (eds) (1983) *The New Christian Right: Mobilization and Legitimation* (New York: Aldine).

LINDBLOM, C. E. and WOODHOUSE, E. J. (1993) *The Policy-Making Process*, 3rd edn (Englewood Cliffs: Prentice Hall).

LIVINGSTONE, D. N. (1987) *Darwin's Forgotten Defenders: The Encounter Between Evangelical Theology and Evolutionary Thought* (Grand Rapids, MI: William B. Eerdmans).

LUGG, C. A. (1994, October) Schools and achieving integrated services: facilitating utilization of the knowledge base. Paper presented at the Annual Meeting of the University Council for Educational Administration, Philadelphia, Pennsylvania.

LUGG, C. A. (1996) *For God and Country: Conservative Ideology and American School Policy* (New York: Peter Lang).

LUGG, C. A. and BOYD, W. L. (1996) Reflections on a Pennsylvania case. *Politics of Education Bulletin,* **23**(3–4), 2–5.

McCARTHY, M. M. (1994) External challenges to public education: values in conflict. Draft of a paper prepared for the American Educational Research Association Meeting, New Orleans.

McLAREN, P. (1993) *Schooling as a Ritual Performance: Towards a Political Economy of Educational Symbols and Gesture,* 2nd edn (New York: Routledge).

McLAREN, P. and SMITH, R. (1989) Televangelism as pedagogy and cultural politics. In H. Giroux and R. Simon (contributors), *Popular Culture, Schooling, and Everyday Life* (New York: Bergin & Garvey).

MURRAY, C. A. (1984) *Losing Ground: American Social Policy, 1950–1980* (New York: Basic Books).

NASH, G. H. (1976) *The Conservative Intellectual Movement in America: Since 1945* (New York: Basic Books).

PAGELS, E. (1988) *Adam, Eve, and the Serpent* (New York: Random House).

PERKINSON, H. J. (1991) *The Imperfect Panacea: American Faith in Education, 1865–1990,* 3rd edn (New York: McGraw-Hill).

PHILLIPS, K. P. (1990) *The Politics of Rich and Poor: Wealth and the American Electorate in the Reagan Aftermath* (New York: Random House).

SILVER, H. (1990) *Education, Change and the Policy Process* (New York: Falmer Press).

SPRING, J. (1994) *The American School: 1642–1993* (New York: McGraw-Hill).

SYKES, S. and BOOTY, J. (eds) (1988) *The Study of Anglicanism* (Philadelphia: SPCK/Fortress Press).

TORBET, R. G. (1950) *A History of the Baptists* (Philadelphia: Judson Press).

TUCK, R. (1991) History of political thought, in P. Burke (ed.), *New Perspectives on Historical Writing* (University Park: Pennsylvania State University Press).

TYSON, L. A. (1986) The US and the world economy in transition. The Berkeley roundtable on the international economy (University of California, Berkeley). BRIE Working Paper No. 22. Paper prepared for the meeting of the Western Economics Association.

VEDLITZ, A. (1988) *Conservative Mythology and Public Policy in America* (New York: Praeger).

WARREN, D. (1983) The federal interest: politics and policy study, in J. H. Best (ed.), *Historical Inquiry in Education, A Research Agenda* (Washington: American Educational Research Association).

WEATHERLY, R. and LIPSKY, M. (1977) Street-level bureaucrats and institutional innovation: implementing special-education reform. *Harvard Educational Review,* **47**(2), 171–197.

WEST, C. (1982) *Prophesy Deliverance!, An Afro-American Revolutionary Christianity* (Philadelphia: Westminster Press).

WIRT, F. M. and KIRST, M. W. (1992) *Schools in Conflict: The Politics of Education,* 3rd edn (Berkeley: McCutchan).

YUDOF, M. G., KIRP, D. L. and LEVIN, B. (1992) *Educational Policy and the Law,* 3rd edn (St Paul, MN: West Publishing Company).

ZAHORCHAK, G. L. (1994) The Politics of Outcome-Based Education in Pennsylvania. Unpublished doctoral dissertation, Pennsylvania State University, University Park.

Index